D0589548

12

12

סיב.

בֿ

2016

ESSENTIAL
RHODES

XB00 000008 0200

Original text by Des Hannigan
Revised and updated by Jane Foster

© AA Media Limited 2008
First published 2008. Revised 2010

ISBN 978-0-7495-6678-4

Published by AA Publishing, a trading name of AA Media Limited, whose registered
office is Fanum House, Basing View, Basingstoke, Hampshire RG21 4EA.
Registered number 06112600.

AA Media Limited retains the copyright in the original edition © 2001 and in all
subsequent editions, reprints and amendments

A CIP catalogue record for this book is available from the British Library

All rights reserved. No part of this publication may be reproduced, stored in a retrieval
system, or transmitted in any form or by any means – electronic, photocopying,
recording or otherwise – unless the written permission of the publishers has been
obtained beforehand. This book may not be sold, resold, hired out or otherwise
disposed of by way of trade in any form of binding or cover other than that in which it
is published, without the prior consent of the publisher. The contents of this publication
are believed correct at the time of printing. Nevertheless, AA Publishing accept no
responsibility for errors, omissions or changes in the details given, or for the
consequences of readers' reliance on this information. This does not affect your
statutory rights. Assessments of attractions, hotels and restaurants are based upon the
author's own experience and contain subjective opinions that may not reflect the
publisher's opinion or a reader's experience. We have tried to ensure accuracy, but
things do change, so please let us know if you have any comments or corrections.

Colour separation by AA Digital Department
Printed and bound in Italy by Printer Trento S.r.l.

A04192
Maps in this title produced from map data © New Holland Publishing (South Africa)
(PTY) Limited 2009

About this book

Symbols are used to denote the following categories:

➕ map reference to maps on cover

✉ address or location

☎ telephone number

🕐 opening times

💷 admission charge

🍴 restaurant or cafe on premises or nearby

Ⓜ nearest underground train station

🚌 nearest bus/tram route

🚆 nearest overground train station

⛴ nearest ferry stop

✈ nearest airport

❓ other practical information

ℹ tourist information office

▶ indicates the page where you will find a fuller description

This book is divided into five sections.

The essence of Rhodes pages 6–19
Introduction; Features; Food and drink and Short break

Planning pages 20–33
Before you go; Getting there; Getting around; Being there

Best places to see pages 34–55
The unmissable highlights of any visit to Rhodes

Best things to do pages 56–71
Great places to have lunch; top beaches; stunning views; places to take the children and more

Exploring pages 72–153
The best places to visit in Rhodes, organized by area

Maps

All map references are to the maps on the covers. For example, Lindos has the reference ➕ J15 – indicating the grid square in which it is to be found

Admission prices

Inexpensive (under €3)
Moderate (€3–€6)
Expensive (over €6)

Hotel prices

Price per double room per night:
€ budget (under €80)
€€ moderate (€80–€160)
€€€ expensive to luxury (over €160)

Restaurant prices

Price for a three-course meal per person without drinks or service:
€ budget (under €15)
€€ moderate (€15–€30)
€€€ expensive (over €30)

Contents

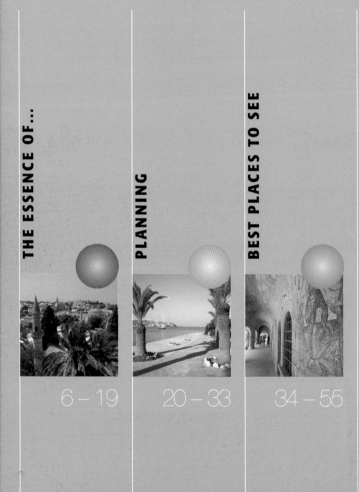

WOLVERHAMPTON PUBLIC LIBRARIES	
XB000000080200	
Bertrams	04/11/2010
914.9587HAN	£5.99
WA	01164825

BEST THINGS TO DO

EXPLORING...

56 – 71   72 – 153

The essence of...

features

Rhodes is the largest and most populated of the islands in the Dodecanese group, in the southeast of the Aegean Sea. It lies only 18km (11 miles) west of the Turkish mainland and can trace its history back to the Stone Age when it was first settled by people from Crete.

Today people arrive here from all over the world, to enjoy its 300 days of sunshine every year, and miles of beaches – the long east coast that runs for about 80km (50 miles) is made up of virtually one beach after another. They appeal very much to the European package holiday market, while Rhodes Town is a big draw for cruise ships sailing between the Mediterranean's major ports.

Unfortunately, in recent years the island has had a bad press because of the drunken exploits of some tourists in a very small number of resorts, Faliraki in particular. The authorities have cracked down on this behaviour, though, and in any case the rest of the island was never affected by it. It still remains a great place for family holidays, and also a good base for those wanting to explore some of the other, smaller islands in the Dodecanese.

Rhodes Town is one of the island's biggest treasures. The Old Town is a UNESCO World Heritage Site, and despite this title it remains very much a lived-in part of the city. In fact it is the largest inhabited medieval town in Europe, a fact that often comes as a surprise to those who only think of sun and sand when they think of Rhodes.

GEOGRAPHY

- Rhodes has an area of about 1,400sq km (540sq miles), much of which is hilly and wooded although most visitors come for the miles of sandy beaches spread out around its 220km (137 miles) of coastline.
- The island's highest point is Mount Attavyros which is 1,215m (3,986ft) high.

POPULATION

Rhodes has a population of about 110,000, and roughly half of these live in the capital. This is usually referred to as Rhodes Town, although over the years it has grown from a town into a city. The old name tends to linger, however.

GOVERNMENT

- Rhodes is an administrative district of Greece and sends elected deputies to the Athens parliament.
- The island is divided into 10 municipal areas, with Rhodes City being the biggest in terms of population.
- There are a further 42 recognized towns and villages on Rhodes.

food & drink

The reputation of Greek food and drink has languished, unfairly, in the shadow of French and Italian cuisine and wine-making. The best Greek tavernas represent the highest standards of traditional cooking, and a modern approach to Greek cuisine is found in many top restaurants, while Rhodes produces some of the best wines in the Mediterranean.

MEZÉDHES (STARTERS)

Making a meal of it in a Greek taverna may mean that you never get past the *mezédhes*. The Greek style of eating *mezédhes* is to order half a dozen mixed plates and then for everyone to dig in. A Greek salad *(horiatiki)* is a good way to start any meal or is just right for a light lunch. The best *horiatiki* are plentiful and comprise a marvellous mix of green salad with cucumber, tomatoes and onions, the whole capped with a generous slice of feta cheese sprinkled with herbs. *Mezédhes* worth trying include *manitaria* (mushrooms), *keftedes* (spicy meatballs), *dolmadakia* (rice wrapped in vine leaves), *kotópoulo* (chicken portions), *saganáki* (fried cheese), *khtapódhi* (octopus), *spanokeftedes* (spinach balls) and *bourekakia* (meat pies). Add to all this a couple of dips such as *tzatziki* (garlic and cucumber yoghurt) or *melitzanosalata* (aubergine and garlic).

MEAT DISHES

Meat dishes on Rhodes follow the Greek standards of moussaka, *souvlaki* (shish kebab with meat, peppers, onions and tomatoes), *pastitsio* (lamb or goat meat with macaroni and tomatoes), *stifádo* (beef stew with tomato sauce and onions) and *padakia* (grilled lamb or goat chops). *Souvlaki* is a good standby, but you might be better settling for chicken (*kotópoulo*) *souvlaki*, because veal or pork on the grill can be tough in some tavernas. Lamb *souvlaki* is tasty but not easily found. Any meat dish that is braised or stewed is usually good.

FISH

Rhodes has always been noted for its fish and the island boasts some outstanding *psarotavernas* (fish restaurants). But overfishing, pollution and a general rise in prices has meant that while the choice is still good, fish dishes can often be very expensive. It is also difficult to know whether fish on offer is locally caught or is imported, frozen or farmed versions. Reasonably priced dishes include

marídhes (whitebait deep-fried in olive oil and sprinkled with lemon), and swordfish, either in meaty steaks or as *xsifhia*, chunks on a kebab. *Kalamarákia* (fried baby squid) is another favourite. Red mullet and lobster tend to be more expensive.

DRINK

Rhodian wines have a good reputation and provided you are not a wine snob, you will enjoy

some excellent vintages from the major island wine producers CAIR and Emery wineries, the latter based at Embonas (► 106). CAIR labels worth trying include Ilios, a dry white wine produced from the Athiri grape; Chevalier de Rhodes, a superior red; and the Moulin range of white, rosé and red wines. Free tastings are available at the CAIR winery, located a couple of kilometres outside Rhodes Town on the Lindos road. Good Emery wines include the Cava red and first-class Chablis-style Villare dry white. Distinctive wines from smaller Rhodian wineries, such as the Anastasia Triantafillou Vineyard (► 130), are available in some island restaurants. Most tavernas have their own house wine, which can often be reasonable. Retsina, resinated white wine, is an acquired taste but the best is excellent. Kourtaki is a decent retsina to try. Light beers and lagers, such as Amstel and the Greek Mythos, are widely available.

short break

If you only have a short time to visit Rhodes, or would like to get a really complete picture of the island, here are the essentials:

● **Spend time on the less-crowded beaches** of the south and west coasts where you will find open spaces and peace and quiet.

● **Wander through Rhodes Old Town** (➤ 50–51 and ➤ 88–89). Take your time and make several visits in order to absorb fully the wonderful atmosphere.

● **Find out if there is a festival or cultural event** being held during your stay and if there is, join in (➤ 24–25).

● **Spend time in Rhodes New Town** (➤ 87) and enjoy the atmosphere of modern, cosmopolitan Greece in cafes and restaurants, and in the fashionable shops.

- **Try to fit in an overnight stay on the island of Symi** (➤ 118–121). A day trip is rewarding, but Symi's old town of Chorio, all steep stone staircases and twisting alleys, is best enjoyed in the cool of evening.

- **Head for the mountains** and visit villages such as Monolithos (➤ 49) or Siana (➤ 148).

- **Always take time to relax at *kafenío* (coffee shop) tables.** Relax, take your time and watch the world go by, but make lively conversation as well.

● **Visit ancient Kamiros** (➤ 46–47) **and Lindos** (➤ 136–141). Both transcend their picture-postcard images. Try to visit as early in the day as possible, when they are less crowded.

● **Explore some of Rhodes' out of the way villages** such as Gennadi (➤ 133) or Lahania (➤ 135). You'll catch the flavour of a quieter, more down-to earth Rhodes.

● **Eat and drink Greek.** Try an assortment of *mezédhes* (starters) – a good selection can make a superb meal in itself and can be quite filling. If you enjoy wine, then try the excellent Rhodian vintages.

Planning

Before you go

WHEN TO GO

JAN	FEB	MAR	APR	MAY	JUN	JUL	AUG	SEP	OCT	NOV	DEC
12°C	12°C	14°C	17°C	22°C	26°C	30°C	29°C	25°C	21°C	18°C	13°C
54°F	54°F	57°F	63°F	72°F	79°F	86°F	84°F	77°F	70°F	64°F	55°F

🌧️ 🌧️ ⛅ ⛅ ☀️ ☀️ ☀️ ☀️ ☀️ ⛅ 🌧️ 🌧️

⬤ High season ⬤ Low season

The vast majority of visitors to Rhodes descend in the summer months, especially in July and August, although this isn't really the ideal time to visit. Daytime temperatures reach into the 30s°C (90s°F), and even higher in recent years when Greece has had summer heatwaves. Even at night the temperature averages 22°C (72°F), which is fine when there's a cooling breeze, but not so fine when the air remains still and sticky.

Although in winter the island seldom sees a frost, the temperature can drop to the low 5–6°C (40s°F) and rain can fall any time between October and March. Unless you do simply want to lie on the beach, the best times to visit are usually April to June, and again from September to about the end of October. In any case this is when the tourist season is starting to wind down, and some establishments will close for winter.

WHAT YOU NEED

		UK	Germany	USA	Netherlands	Spain
●	Required					
○	Suggested	Some countries require a passport to remain valid for a minimum period (usually at least six months) beyond the date of entry – contact their consulate or embassy or your travel agency for details.				
▲	Not required					

	UK	Germany	USA	Netherlands	Spain
Passport valid for 6 months beyond date of departure	●	●	●	●	●
Visa (regulations can change – check before booking your trip)	▲	▲	▲	▲	▲
Onward or return ticket	▲	▲	▲	▲	▲
Health inoculations	▲	▲	▲	▲	▲
Health documentation (➤ 23, Health Insurance)	●	●	●	●	●
Travel insurance	●	●	●	●	●
Driving license (current or international)	●	●	●	●	●
Car insurance certificate (if own car)	●	●	●	●	●
Car registration document (if own car)	●	●	●	●	●

WEBSITES

Greek National Tourist Board:
www.gnto.gr
www.gnto.co.uk

Additional websites:
www.agrotravel.gr

www.andotravel.gr/eot
www.barefoot.info
www.gtp.gr
www.rhodes.gr/portal_en/index.php
www.rhodesguide.com/

TOURIST OFFICES AT HOME

In the UK
Greek National Tourism
Organization (GNTO)
4 Conduit Street
London W1R 0DJ
☎ 020 7495 9300

In the USA
Greek National Tourism
Organization (GNTO)
Olympic Tower
645 Fifth Avenue
New York, NY 10022
☎ 212/421-5777

In the Netherlands
Grieske Nationale
Organizatie voor
Toerisme
Kerkstatt
1017 GC Amsterdam
☎ 020 6248786

HEALTH INSURANCE

EU nationals can get medical treatment with the relevant documentation
(EHIC card for Britons), although private medical insurance is still advised
and is essential for other visitors. Visitors from the US should check their
insurance coverage.

Dental treatment is not available free of charge and should be covered
by your personal medical insurance. Check with the Tourist Police or at
your hotel for the name of the nearest dentist. Have a check-up before
leaving home.

TIME DIFFERENCES

GMT	Rhodes	Germany	USA (NY)	Netherlands	Spain
12 noon	2PM	1PM	7AM	1PM	1PM

Rhodes is two hours ahead of Greenwich Mean Time (GMT +2). The
clocks go forward one hour on the last Sunday in March and back one
hour on the last Sunday in October.

NATIONAL HOLIDAYS

1 Jan *New Year's Day*
6 Jan *Epiphany*
Feb/Mar *'Clean Monday'*
25 Mar *Independence Day*
Mar/Apr *Good Friday and Easter Monday*
1 May *May Day*

May/Jun *Ascension Day*
15 Aug *Feast of the Assumption*
28 Oct *Óchi Day*
25 Dec *Christmas Day*
26 Dec *St Stephen's Day*

Restaurants and some tourist shops may stay open on these days, but museums will be closed.

WHAT'S ON WHEN

January *6 Jan – Epiphany.* Service in Cathedral of St John the Evangelist, Rhodes Town. Blessing of the sea water at Mandraki Harbour, when a priest throws a crucifix into the water and youngsters dive in for the honour of retrieving it.

February–March *Pre-Lenten Carnival.* During the weeks before the beginning of Lent, various carnivals are staged on Rhodes. Sunday before Lent: carnival processions and fancy dress in Rhodes Old Town and at Archangelos, Appolona, Afandou, Ialyssos and Kamiros Skala. Following day: *Kathari Deftera,* "Clean Monday", when families and friends head for the countryside and beaches to picnic and to fly kites.
7 Mar – Dodecanese Reunification Day. Celebrates reunification with Greece in 1947. Parade in Rhodes Town. Theatre performances.
25 Mar – Greek Independence Day.

Easter (date variable) Most important festival of Greek Orthodoxy (► opposite). Expect explosive firecrackers over Easter weekend. Symi has its own very characteristic celebrations.

May *1 May – May Day.* Country picnics; garlands of flowers brought back to decorate doorways and balconies.

June *24 Jun – Feast of St John the Baptist.* Bonfires and parties.

July *First week of Jul – Naval Week.* Concerts, fireworks and boat races.
20 Jul – Feast of Profitis Ilias. Large numbers of people assemble at the mountain of Profitis Ilias to celebrate feast day of Prophet Elijah.
30 Jul – Lively celebrations at the village of Soroni in honour of St Paul.

August Dance festivals at various villages throughout the month.
6 Aug – Religious festival on Chalki; traditional mock battles, with the throwing of flour and eggs.

15 Aug – Assumption (Dormition) of the Blessed Virgin Mary. Very important week-long festival, during which many Greeks return to their native island and village.

September *8 Sep – Birth of the Virgin.* Unique event at Tsambika, when women wishing to conceive make a special pilgrimage to the hilltop monastery church (➤ 125).

October *28 Oct – Óchi Day ("No" Day).* Patriotic celebration of Greece's refusal to capitulate to demands of Mussolini in 1940. Parades, folk dancing, speeches and general celebrations.

November *8 Nov – Feast of the Archangels Michael and Gabriel.* Religious celebrations and festivities at Archangelos, and at monastery of Panormitis on the island of Symi.

EASTER CELEBRATIONS

Easter is the major festival of the religious year. On Good Friday evening church ceremonies begin, both inside the churches and outside as solemn processions move through the streets. On Holy Saturday night the most powerful ceremony takes place and culminates with great bursts of fireworks in the streets as Christ is declared "risen". People flow from the churches bearing lit candles which they try to keep alight until they reach home. There are early breakfast feasts on Sunday morning and then general feasting throughout the day. Churches are always packed but people gather outside as well. Remember to dress appropriately if you attend a church service.

Getting there

BY AIR

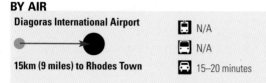

Diagoras International Airport

15km (9 miles) to Rhodes Town

📷 N/A

🚌 N/A

🚗 15–20 minutes

The majority of flights to Rhodes are charter flights from cities all over Europe, operating roughly from Easter to October, the peak holiday season. During these summer months there are regular flights from Rhodes to Crete and other Greek islands. There are also year-round scheduled flights to Athens, from where there are daily onward flights to Rhodes, usually several each day. These are operated by both Olympic Air (tel: 210 3550 500; www.olympicair.com) and Aegean Airlines (tel: 210 626 1000; www.aegeanair.com).

BY FERRY

Ferries operate throughout the year between Athens and Rhodes, some calling at other Dodecanese islands and others sailing via the Cyclades. There are also faster ferries from Rhodes to the other Dodecanese islands, to Crete and to some of the other island groups. For further details see the website of the Greek Travel Pages (www.gtp.gr), which includes ferry timetables and a ticket booking service.

Getting around

PUBLIC TRANSPORT

Internal flights Domestic flights are operated by Olympic Air
☎ 210 3550 500 (Athens) and by Aegean Airways ☎ 210 626 1000 (Athens) or 22410 98345 (Rhodes). Domestic flight tickets are non-transferable. All flights are non-smoking. Flights are often well-booked in advance. Reserve seats in advance and confirm within five days of your flight.

Trains There are no train services on Rhodes.

Buses The national bus company, KTEL (Kratiko Tamio Ellinikon Leoforion), serves the east coast of Rhodes from a bus stand in Papagou Street, just up from Rimini Square. The municipal bus service RODA serves the west coast from a stand in Averof Street behind the arcades of the New Market. There are timetables at the stand kiosks and tourist offices.

Boat trips Ferries run between Rhodes Town and Pireas (Athens) at least once a day (more often in summer). The trip can take up to 18 hours. Ferries run between Rhodes and the other Dodecanese islands and to Crete. Ferries from Rhodes to Pireas stop at several islands in the Cyclades en route (notably Santorini and Milos). Finding out about ferries can be frustrating, because rival agencies supply information only about the companies they represent. Ask at as many agencies as possible. Pleasure boats operate from Mandraki Harbour on day trips to Symi and Turkey and to various resorts, including Lindos.

Urban transport Town buses Nos 2–6 leave from a stand opposite the main entrance to the New Market on Eleftherias. Only useful if you wish to travel outside the immediate limits of the New Town and Old Town.

TAXIS
The central taxi rank in Rhodes Town is at Rimini Square ☎ 22410 27666. Call radio cabs on ☎ 22410 64712/64790. Boards indicating fares to main resorts and tourist sites are displayed at various points.

FARES AND TICKETS
Travelling in Rhodes is much less expensive than in many other European destinations and there is a good bus network. Even taxis are used frequently because fares are reasonably inexpensive and when a few people are sharing they represent a viable alternative. In Rhodes Town and one or two other larger places you should buy your bus ticket in advance from the bus station or ticket kiosk, but in smaller places you buy your ticket from the driver as you board. There are some concessionary fares for young children, students and elderly people.

DRIVING

Bus services on Rhodes are generally reliable, but a hire car is the best way of exploring the rural areas. There are numerous rental options ranging from international names to local outfits, many of which offer reasonable deals. Always check round the vehicle for existing dents or scratches. Be aware that some Rhodian roads, indicated on maps as being surfaced, can turn out to be thudding nightmares of potholes and vestigial tarmac. Drive extremely slowly at night: deep holes, and even road works, are not always clearly signed. Be wary in a stand-off at constricted sections of road, especially if an oncoming vehicle waves you on – the local driver behind you may already be pulling out impatiently, and probably into your side, as you pull out. Flashing headlights mean that the approaching driver is coming ahead, not that he is inviting you to do so.

- Speed limit on national highways: 100kph (62mph)
  Speed limit on main roads: 80kph (50mph)
  Speed limit in built-up areas: 50kph (31mph)
- Seatbelts must be worn in front seats and in the rear where fitted. Children under 10 years are not allowed in the front seat.
- Drink-driving is heavily penalized. There is random breath-testing. Never drive under the influence of alcohol.
- Petrol *(venzini)* is usually available in five grades: super *(sooper)*, regular *(apli)*, unleaded *(amolyvdhi)*, super unleaded *(sooper amolyvdhi)*, and confusingly, *petrelaio*, which is diesel. Petrol stations are normally open 7–7 (closed Sun); larger ones (often self-service) are open 24 hours. Most take credit cards. There are few petrol stations in remote areas.
- If you break down driving your own car then the Automobile and Touring Club of Greece (ELPA) provide 24-hour road assistance (☎ 10400). If the car is hired, follow the instructions given in the documentation; most international rental firms provide a rescue service.

CAR RENTAL

Most of the leading rental companies have offices in the main towns and at the airport, and even resorts will probably have a few local hire firms. Car hire in Rhodes is expensive, however, and accident rates are high.

Being there

TOURIST OFFICES

The Greek National Tourist Office (EOT) is on the corner of Papágou and Makariou streets in Rhodes Town ☎ 22410 44330. There is also a municipal tourist office in Rimini Square, which is open daily June–September ☎ 22410 35945.

In smaller towns and resorts around the island, travel agencies also function as tourist information centres. As well as booking car and scooter hire, tours, boat trips and the like, staff can also answer questions about local attractions and activities, suggest scenic walks and can often help you find accommodations in the area if you haven't pre-booked.

You can also get information and help from the Rhodes Tourist Police (Kapathou 1, Rhodes Town ☎ 22410 23329). As everywhere in Greece, this is a separate branch of the police which concentrates on the needs of tourists, checks restaurant and hotel prices, and provides information to visitors. Many officers also speak a foreign language and are happy to be of assistance.

MONEY

Greece's currency is the euro (€), which is divided into 100 cents. Coins come in denominations of 1, 2, 5, 10, 20 and 50 cents and €1 and €2. Notes come in denominations of €5, €10, €20, €50, €100, €200 and €500. Major credit cards are accepted in the larger and more expensive hotels, shops and restaurants, but otherwise cash is still the preferred method of payment in Rhodes.

TIPS/GRATUITIES

Yes ✓   No ✗

Restaurants (service not included)	✓	10%
Cafes/bars (service not included)	✓	Discretionary
Tour guides	✓	Discretionary
Taxis	✓	change
Porters	✓	€1
Chambermaids	✓	€1
Cloakroom attendants	✓	€0.50
Toilets	✗	

POSTAL AND INTERNET SERVICES

Post Offices are identified by a yellow "OTE" sign. Shops and kiosks often sell stamps along with postcards. Postboxes are yellow. Post offices are generally open Mon–Fri 8–8.

Internet cafes can be found in the main towns and resorts around the island. In Rhodes Town try Control Internet Cafe, Alexandrou Diakou 44 Street ☎ 22410 24564.

TELEPHONES

International Direct Dialling is available throughout Rhodes. Calls can be made using a phone card in a telephone booth. Cards can be bought from kiosks, OTE offices and some shops.

International dialling codes
From Rhodes to:
UK: 00 44
Germany: 00 49
USA and Canada: 00 1
Netherlands: 00 31

Emergency telephone numbers
Police 100
Fire 199
Ambulance 166
Forest Fire 191

EMBASSIES AND CONSULATES

UK: ☎ 22410 22005
USA: ☎ 210 721 2951 (Athens)
France: ☎ 22410 22318

Germany: ☎ 22410 37125
Netherlands: ☎ 22410 31571

HEALTH ADVICE

Sun advice Rhodes enjoys sunshine for most of the year, and from May until September it is almost constant. During July and August, when the sun is at its hottest, a hat, strong-protection suncream and plenty of water are recommended.

Drugs Pharmacies *(farmakía)*, indicated by a green cross sign, can give advice and prescriptions for common ailments. If you need prescription drugs, take the exact details from home. Most pharmacies have someone who can speak English.

Safe water Tap water is regarded as safe to drink. Bottled water is cheap to buy and is widely available. Drink plenty of water during hot weather.

PERSONAL SAFETY

Rhodes is safe generally, but crime is on the increase, especially in crowded places. Report any problems to the Tourist Police, who can often speak several languages.

● Leave money and valuables in your hotel safe.
● Carry only what you need and keep it hidden.
● Try not to attract the attention of pickpockets.
● Always lock car doors and never leave valuables visible inside.

Tourist Police assistance: ☎ 22410 23329

ELECTRICITY

The power supply in Rhodes is 200 volts AC, 50Hz. Sockets accept two-pin round plugs. Visitors from the UK require a plug adaptor and US visitors will need a transformer for appliances operating on 100–120 volts.

OPENING HOURS

● Shops   ● Museums/Monuments   ● Pharmacies
● Banks   ● Churches

9 AM	10 AM	11 AM	12 PM	1 PM	2 PM	3 PM	4 PM	5 PM	6 PM
9.30	10.30	11.30	12.30	1.30	2.30	3.30	4.30	5.30	

In addition to the general times shown above, many shops in tourist areas stay open daily from 8am until late evening. Banks are closed at the weekend and on public holidays. Opening hours of museums and archaeological sites vary enormously, with many national museums being closed on Mondays. Some restaurants operate seasonal opening times.

LANGUAGE

The official language of Rhodes is Greek. Many of the locals speak English, but a few words of Greek can be useful in rural areas where locals may know no English. It is also useful to know the Greek alphabet – particularly for reading street names and road signs. A few useful words and phrases are listed below, with phonetic transliterations and accents to show emphasis.

yes	*né*	I don't understand	*katalavéno*
no	*óhi*		*…adío or yásas*
please	*parakaló*	goodbye	*yásoo*
thank you	*efharistó*	sorry	*signómi*
hello	*yásas, yásoo*	you're welcome	*parakaló*
good morning	*kalí méra*	where is...?	*poú eené..?*
good evening	*kalí spéra*	help!	*voíthia!*
good night	*kalí níkhta*	my name is...	*meh léne*
excuse me	*me sinchoríte*	I don't speak Greek	*then miló helliniká*

hotel	*xenodhohío*	toilet	*twaléta*
room	*dhomátyo*	bath	*bányo*
...single/double	*monó/dhipló*	shower	*doos*
for three people	*ya tría átoma*	hot water	*zestó neró*
breakfast	*proinó*	key	*klidhí*
guesthouse	*pansyón*	towel	*petséta*

bank	*trápeza*	exchange rate	*isotimía*
exchange office	*ghrafío*	credit card	*pistotikí kárta*
	sinalághmatos	traveller's cheque	*taxidhyotikí epitayí*
post office	*tahidhromío*	passport	*dhiavatíryn*
money	*leftá*	cheap	*ftinós*
how much?	*póso káni?*	expensive	*akrivós*

restaurant	*estiatório*	dessert	*epidhórpyo*
cafe	*kafenío*	table	*trapézi*
menu	*menóo*	the bill	*loghariazmós*
lunch	*yévma*	bread	*psomi*
dinner	*dhípno*	water	*nero*

wine	*krasi*	toilet	*twaléta*
coffee	*kafés*	waiter/waitress	*garsóni/servitóra*
fruit	*fróoto*	tea (black)	*tsái*
aeroplane	*aeropláno*	...port/harbour	*limáni*
airport	*aerodhrómio*	single ticket	*apló*
bus	*leoforío*	return ticket	*isitírio metepistrofís*
...station	*stathmós*	car	*aftokínito*
...stop	*stási*	taxi	*taxí*
boat	*karávi*	timetable	*dhromolóyo*
		petrol	*venzíni*

GREEK ALPHABET

The Greek alphabet cannot be transliterated into other languages in a straightforward way. This can lead to variations in romanized spellings of Greek words and place-names. It also leads inevitably to inconsistencies, especially when comparing different guide books, leaflets and signs. However, the differences rarely make any name unrecognizable. The language looks complex, but it is worth memorizing the alphabet to help with signs, destinations and so on.

Alpha	Αα	*short a, as in hat*	Pi	Ππ	*p sound*
Beta	Ββ	*v sound*	Rho	Ρρ	*r sound*
Gamma	Γγ	*guttural g sound*	Sigma	Σσ	*s sound*
Delta	Δδ	*hard th, as in father*	Tau	Ττ	*t sound*
Epsilon	Εε	*short e, as in egg*	Upsilon	Υυ	*ee, or y as in funny*
Zita	Ζζ	*z sound*	Phi	Φφ	*f sound*
Eta	Ηη	*long e, as in feet*	Chi	Χχ	*guttural ch, as in loch*
Theta	Θθ	*soft th, as in think*	Psi	Ψψ	*ps, as in chops*
Iota	Ιι	*short i, as in hit*	Omega	Ωω	*long o, as in bone*
Kappa	Κκ	*k sound*			
Lambda	Λλ	*l sound*			
Mu	Μμ	*m sound*			
Nu	Νν	*n sound*			
Xi	Ξξ	*x or ks sound*			
Omicron	Οο	*short o, as in pot*			

Best places to see

1 Akropoli, Lindos

Situated on a spectacular hill, the Acropolis is a potent mix of ancient Greek antiquities and Byzantine and medieval buildings.

The 114m-high (374ft) Acropolis hill of Lindos dominates the coast to north and south. The low-lying neck of land behind the Acropolis sparkles with the white-painted houses of the medieval village of Lindos (➤ 136–138). The Sanctuary of Athena Lindia was established on the Acropolis in the 2nd millennium BC and today is one of its finest restorations. Later additions included a large *stoa*

(colonnaded avenue), vaults and cisterns. Substantial fortifications were added during the Byzantine period, as was the Church of St John that stands inside the Acropolis.

Stones from the ancient structures were used by the Knights of St John to repair and expand the Byzantine fortress. The Italians carried out substantial reconstruction during the early 20th century, but their methods and materials were often inadequate, and today there is a continuing refurbishment that accounts for the often frustrating presence of scaffolding and machinery. Make your way up the path past the souvenir sellers, and take a deep breath before you tackle the steep approach steps. Pick your way carefully through the darkened vault of the Knights' Hall, climb in brilliant sunlight to the terrace and up the monumental staircase, then wander amid this glorious open-air museum of Aegean history, with superb views as a bonus.

➕ J15 ✉ 48km (30 miles) south of Rhodes Town ☎ 22410 31258 ⏱ Jul–Oct Mon 1–7:30, Tue–Sun 8–7:30; Nov–Jun Tue–Sun 8:30–3 ✋ Expensive 🍽 Snack bar at entrance (€€) 🚌 East side bus, Rhodes–Lindos, daily (Rimini Square) ⛴ Summer excursion ferries daily from Mandraki Harbour ℹ Main Square, Lindos

2 Anaktoro ton Arkhonton (Palace of the Grand Masters)

The Palace of the Grand Masters, in Rhodes Town, is an impressive monumental building, a 1930s Italian reconstruction of the medieval original.

The 15th-century Knights of St John built their Palace of the Grand Masters on the roots of a decaying Byzantine fortress. The building remained the focus of the Collachium, the inner fortress of the Knights, until the Turkish conquest of 1522. In 1856 the palace was demolished by an accidental explosion of stored munitions. It was a sorry ruin that the Italians tried to recreate in its medieval form, although their choice of materials proved to be less than durable, and their methods less than responsible. Numerous ancient artefacts were dumped in the new foundations.

Today the palace houses two outstanding museum collections on its ground floor: the Ancient Rhodes Exhibition (➤ 76) and the Medieval Exhibition (➤ 76). From the cool shade of the palace's entrance portal, you emerge into the harsh white light of the inner courtyard; it is lined with cloisters and arches, some holding Hellenistic statues transferred from Kos by the Italians. A grand staircase leads from the left of the entrance portal to a circuit of upper chambers, paved with Hellenistic, Roman and early Christian mosaics and marble inlays, also from Kos. Look for superb examples in the Chamber of the Sea Horse and Nymph, in the Dolphin Chamber, and in the corridor where Poseidon defeats the giant Polybotes.

✚ *Rhodes Town d5*

✉ Plateia Kleovoulou ☎ 22410 65270

🕐 Apr–Oct Tue–Sun 8:30–8; Nov–Mar Tue–Sun 8:30–3:30 (hours can be flexible, especially during peak season) ✋ Expensive

🍴 Cafe on site (€€)

3 Asklipio

The remote inland village of Asklipio boasts two splendid Byzantine monuments: the Church of the Dormition of the Virgin and the castle ruins.

The superb church dates from 1060, and was built over an existing basilica. Its cruciform shape is supplemented by two additional apses. Built of warm, honey-coloured stone with a red-tiled dome and barrel roofs, there is a separate bell-tower gateway. Inside the church is a feast of 17th-century frescoes. The frescoes are narrative in style and illustrate Old Testament themes such as the Genesis sequence and the story of Daniel and the Lion. The splendid *hokhláki* (pebble mosaic) floor has a big star motif in front of the altar, and from the central dome there hangs a truly awesome chandelier. Alongside the church are two small museums, one displaying religious items, the other a collection of rural artefacts including oil pressing equipment.

A signposted road leads up to the castle from whose ruinous battlements there are fine views across the inland *maquis*-smothered hills and east towards the sea. The castle is well protected by natural rock outcrops, and by jagged fangs of rock that would have formed a natural barrier in their own right. The interior of the castle is overgrown, and you may stumble on the occasional carcass of a sheep or goat. There is a narrow inner parapet round the walls, and ancient water tanks, sunk into the ground, are in an unprotected condition.

➕ F5 ✉ 65km (40 miles) south of Rhodes Town ⏱ Church, daily 9–6 in summer; varies in winter. Services are held at various times. Museums, same hours as church. Castle, open access 🏛 Church and museums inexpensive, castle free 🍴 Agapitos Taverna (€) 🚌 East side bus, Rhodes–Asklipio turn-off, then 4km (2.5-mile) uphill walk to village, daily (Rimini Square) ❓ Saint's Day Festival, 15 Aug. Please do not enter church wearing shorts or revealing tops. Avoid casual visits during services

4 Ialyssos

The ancient city of Ialyssos once stood on the slopes of 267m-high (876ft) Mount Filerimos. Today the site contains outstanding archaeological artefacts.

The golden-walled Church of Our Lady was built originally by the Knights of St John, and was restored during the early 20th century by the Italians. Internally, it is an exquisite cluster of cool hexagonal chambers, each with groin vaulting. Behind the church is a colonnaded courtyard with monastic cells, linked to a two-storeyed abbot's quarters. In front of the church's handsome bell-tower is a sunken baptismal font dating from a 5th- to 6th-century Christian basilica. Immediately outside the church's entrance door lie the excavated foundations of a 3rd century BC Temple

of Athena, successor to an even earlier Phoenician temple. It is the most poignant feature of the hilltop, and offers a tantalizing indication of what else may lie buried under here.

Beyond all this lie the cliff-edge ruins of a Byzantine fortress that was used in turn by the Knights of St John, the Turks and the Italians, and then was bombed by Allied forces during World War II. Among other features on Filerimos is the chapel of Agios Georgios

Hostos, sunk into the hillside just to the left of the entrance booth. The chapel contains rather faded, but still impressive, medieval frescoes. To the west of the cafe, an Italian-era "Calvary" avenue, hooded by trees and flanked by rather grim Stations of the Cross, leads arrow-straight to a monumental cross, 17m (56ft) high and with an internal staircase leading to viewing areas in the cross's arms.

✚ K23 ✉ 10km (6 miles) southwest of Rhodes Town
☎ 22410 92202 🕐 Jul–Oct daily 8–7:30; Nov–Jun daily 8:30–3 💷 Moderate 🍴 Cafe/shop on site (€€) 🚌 West side bus, Rhodes–Paradissi, daily (Averof Street), to Trianda only, then 5km (3 miles) to site

5 Ippoton (Street of the Knights)

The famous "medieval" Street of the Knights in Rhodes Town is a set-piece Italian restoration of the enclave created by the Knights of St John as their main thoroughfare.

Ippoton is a beautiful urban street, a portrait in warm stone and close-knit cobbling. It descends to the east from the entrance gate of the Palace of the Grand Masters and has a formal stillness that is barely relieved during the day by clusters of visitors listening with hushed intent to their tour guides. The

buildings contain splendid interiors, but most are occupied by municipal and cultural organizations and are not open to the public, unless by special arrangement. Absence of commercial outlets has preserved the street's architectural integrity, but its modern appearance gives no flavour of its probable medieval vigour and clutter. The Knights kept their horses in ground floor stables here.

The Knights were organized by their countries of origin and their language into national groups called "Tongues". Each Tongue had its own establishment or "Inn", where meetings were held and where guests were accommodated. Many of the Inns are located in Ippoton, including the Inns of Provence and of Spain and the impressive Inn of the Tongue of France, located about midway down the north side of the street. This building is notable for its arched doorways, turreted battlements and crocodile waterspouts. Throughout the street, marble reliefs displaying coats of arms disturb the flat rigour of the buildings' facades. Here and there, dim alleyways lead off from the south side of Ippoton towards the commercial frenzy of the neighbouring shopping street of Sokratous, a striking contrast to the hush of Ippoton.

✚ *Rhodes Town d6* ✉ Rhodes Old Town ⓚ Open access
🍴 Several cafes in Orfeos at west end (€–€€)

6 Kamiros

Ancient Kamiros is one of the most pleasing ruins of Mediterranean antiquity, reflecting a period when Greek civilization was at its apogee.

Kamiros has an idyllic location on a pine-covered hillside above the sea. The settlement probably originated in the 2nd millennium BC, but flourished during the period 1000 to 400BC. It was devastated by an earthquake in 226BC, but was rebuilt. A later earthquake in AD142 led to a final abandonment. Kamiros is a glorious reminder of the balance and serenity of urban planning in Hellenistic Greece, and is a persuasive argument in favour of the period being designated a true "Golden Age".

The site lies within a south-facing terraced amphitheatre, partially excavated from a hillside. The central street rises from the lowest area of public buildings around Agora Square. These included an *agorá*, or market building, Doric and Ionic temples, a sanctuary with altars, a bath house, and Fountain Square, with its columns partially restored. The level above is filled with the ruins of houses, units of which are separated by narrow alleyways. To the right, a restored stone staircase leads up from the public area to the upper level, where the Acropolis was sited and where the foundations of a sacred precinct, a temple and a *stoa* (colonnaded avenue) survive today. Try to visit either early or late in the day, to avoid the large number of coach parties that invariably arrive by late morning.

✚ E12 ✉ 34km (21 miles) southwest of Rhodes Town ☎ 22410 40037
🕓 Jul–Oct Tue–Sun 8–7:30; Nov–Jun Tue–Sun 8:30–3 💷 Moderate 🍴 Taverna Old Kamiros (€; ➤ 129), seasonal cafe (€€), tavernas (€) at coast road access 🚌 West side bus, Rhodes–Kamiros, daily (Averof Street), to coast road turn-off only. 1km (0.6 miles) uphill to site

7 # Kastrou Monolithos

This spectacular medieval castle, perched high on a rocky pinnacle, offers superb views over a landscape of forested mountains and wild coastline.

The castle of Monolithos stands on top of an enormous crag called Monopetra that rises to a height of 236m (774ft) from pine-covered slopes above Kerameni Bay. The castle dates from 1476 and was a stronghold of the Knights of St John,

built on top of an existing Byzantine fortress. Its broken walls shelter a ruined basilica and the intact church of St Panteleimon. The castle is easily reached from roadside parking by following a path that leads through pines to a fine stone staircase. High cliffs drop away on three sides of the castle, so take great care when near the edge. There are exhilarating views of the island of Chalki (► 132) and of the coast to the north.

The road leading on from the castle descends for 5km (3 miles) through an astonishing series of bends to reach the remote, south-facing Fourni beach. On the east side of a projecting rock headland, reached by rough steps and a path from the far end of the beach, are manmade caves, probably carved out by fishermen at some time in the past but also said to have contained ancient burials, and now revered as holy grottoes. Steps lead down to a sea-washed pit, known locally as The Queen's Bath, but more probably an old sluice-pot, used by fishermen for storing shellfish. The nearby village of Monolithos is an unassuming, friendly place with a long history of survival against the odds, including strong resistance to the German occupation of 1943–45.

➕ B7 ✉ On the west coast, 55km (34 miles) southwest of Rhodes Town ⏰ Open access 💰 Free 🍴 Seasonal *kantiná* (food and drink stall) at approach to castle and Fourni beach (€) 🚌 West side bus, Rhodes–Monolithos, daily (Averof Street), to Monolithos village only

8 Palia Poli (Old Town)

Rhodes Old Town is a medieval fortress town of such historical value that it was declared a World Heritage Site by UNESCO in 1988.

The Old Town of Rhodes is contained within the 4km (2.5 miles) of defensive walls that the Knights of St John built on Byzantine fortifications. Within the walls lie remains of Hellenistic, Roman, Byzantine and Moorish buildings. The Knights divided their city into two enclaves. In the higher northwestern section lay the Collachium, the castle, in which stood the Palace of the Grand Masters (➤ 38–39), the administrative buildings and dwellings of the Order. The rest of the town was the Hora, or Burg, where the merchants and working population lived.

Today the Collachium incorporates the carefully preserved monumental buildings of the Knights, impressive, but slightly sterile, museum pieces. It is the Hora, the Lower Town, that captivates with its dark sandstone and limestone buildings, occasional walls vivid with ochre and sea blue paint, and all crammed within a tangled web of cobbled lanes, many of which are braced throughout their lengths with flying arches intended to minimise earthquake damage. Everywhere, tree-shaded squares and courtyards punctuate the maze. No building replicates another amid this marvellous scrabble of jostling houses, dilapidated mosques, tiny Byzantine churches, ancient foundations, ornamental doorways, *hokhláki* (pebble mosaic) paving and dusty lost corners.

Ten gates in the encircling walls give access from the New Town and harbour areas to this marvellous enclave. The monumental areas of Ippoton (Street of the Knights, ➤ 44–45) and the Palace of the Grand Masters are easily explored, but while wandering through the Old Town it can be easy to miss some outstanding corners. Rewarding places to search out are the ancient streets of Omirou, Ippodamou, Pythagora, and especially Agios Fanouriou. A walk along the Old Town walls is recommended (➤ 90–91) for an overview of the dense jigsaw of buildings and alleyways, and the defensive works of the outer walls and moat (➤ 82).

The Old Jewish Quarter (➤ 80) occupies the most easterly section of the Old Town and is often the busiest area. It is the first stop for cruise ship visitors and leads seamlessly into the thronging Sokratous Street, the Old Town's shopping mall. The competing tavernas, restaurants, cafes, souvenir shops, and the chattering bottlenecks of popular shopping areas are entirely in keeping with the Old Town's centuries of raucous commercial life.

✚ *Rhodes Town e6* 🍴 Alexis Taverna (€€€; ➤ 58), Yiannis Taverna (€; ➤ 97) ❓ Pre-Lenten Carnival (➤ 24) ℹ Rimini Square ☎ 22410 35945

Petaloudes

Petaloudes is Rhodes' famous "Valley of the Butterflies", where swarms of Jersey tiger moths settle each summer in order to breed.

Petaloudes is a relentlessly popular tourist destination that attracts vast numbers of coach tours and individual visitors as much as it does its moths; or "butterflies" as they are called for publicity reasons. The moths gather at Petaloudes from late June to September, attracted by the shade and humidity of the stream-fed woods and the resin of the numerous liquid amber trees in the valley. They cover the trunks of the trees and the surfaces of stream-side rocks with a cloak of yellow and black wings, relieved by occasional blinks of red underwing.

Petaloudes lies in a wooded fold of the hills that run southwest from Rhodes Town. The path

through the upper and lower valley is landscaped, surfaced and linked by rustic bridges and stairways. Conspicuous signs, and an increased control by the site management, remind visitors that disturbance of the moths is stressful to them and can disrupt the mating cycle.

Outside the main "butterfly" months of June to September, the valley is still a pleasantly wooded escape from the beaches and the sun's glare, even although the main attraction is absent. At any time of the year, the valley above the upper road offers a pleasant uphill walk of just under 1km (0.6 miles) to the little monastery church of Panagia Kalopetra on the road above.

✠ J21 ✉ 25km (15 miles) southwest of Rhodes Town ☎ 22410 81801 🕐 May–Sep daily 8–7. Upper valley is accessible all year ✋ Moderate (less when there are few moths present) 🍴 Taverna/cafes on site (€€) 🚌 West side bus, Rhodes–Petaloudes, daily (Averof Street)

10 Profitis Ilias

The wooded mountain of Profitis Ilias rises to a height of 798m (2,618ft) and there are magnificent views from the top.

Today Profitis Ilias is a forested enclave with a mix of mainly Calabrian pines, cedars and oaks. In the 1930s, the Italian occupiers of the island set about transforming the forested ridge of the mountain into a semi-wild park, attracted perhaps by the sub-Alpine nature of the terrain. The ruins and remains of this era are a telling comment on the fate of fascist ambition, yet much of the Italian landscaping still enhances Profitis Ilias in contrast to the ugly clusters of communication aerials and buildings that crowd its off-limits summit.

The road that climbs the mountain's wooded slopes from Salakos in the west is a serpentine delight (▶ 70). If you approach from Eleoussa in the east, you pass the charming little Byzantine church of Agios Nikolaos Fountoukli in its peaceful roadside setting. The church contains some fine, if faded, medieval frescoes. Both approaches lead eventually to a junction, high amid the pines, but below the true summit. Here stands the Italian era, chalet-style hotel Elafos and its annexe, Elafina. The complex is no longer used. Alongside is the Church of Profítis Ilias. There is car parking by the old hotel and at the roadside near the old stable building which now houses a basic *kafenío* (cafe/coffee shop). A rough track leads higher up the mountain, but there are old pathways through the woods that make for enjoyable walking (➤ 116–117).

✚ F10 ✉ 50km (31 miles) southwest of Rhodes Town ⊙ Open access 🍴 Seasonal *kafenío* (€) 🚌 West side bus, Rhodes–Salakos, daily (Averof Street). There is a steep path leading up to Profitis Ilias from Salakos. Allow 1.5 hours ❓ Feast of Profitis Ilias, 20 Jul. The area is very popular on *Kathari Deftera*, "Clean Monday", the Monday before Ash Wednesday

Best things to do

Great places to have lunch

Alexis Taverna (€€€)

A Rhodes favourite for over 40 years, still producing new recipes as well as simple fish grilled to perfection. Very laid-back atmosphere.

✉ Sokratous 18, Rhodes Old Town ☎ 22410 29347

Antique Restaurant (€€)

A couple of blocks back from Elli Beach, serving a vast range of traditional Greek meat and fish dishes, plus pizza and pasta. There's live music, singing and dancing most days.

✉ Iroon Politehniou 14, Rhodes New Town ☎ 22410 23974
☎ www.restaurantantique.com

Argo (€€)

This fine restaurant has a prime position on a rocky promontory at the quiet southern end of Haraki beach. Service is excellent with a good range of dishes. Local fish is a speciality.

✉ Haraki, Northern Rhodes ☎ 22440 51410;
www.argorestaurant.gr

Bakis Taverna (€)

A favourite Sunday lunchtime venue with locals, renowned for its excellent meats. Diners choose the cuts they want, which are then cooked on a barbeque and served on a big platter at the tables.

✉ Embonas, Northern Rhodes ☎ 22460 41442

Epta Piges (€€)

Set in a clearing amid pinewoods and next to a trickling stream, this much-loved eatery offers authentic Greek cooking.

✉ Archangelos, Northern Rhodes ☎ 22410 56259;
www.eptapiges.com

Kozas Taverna (€€–€€€)

Dating back to 1932, this long-standing seafood restaurant serves fresh fish on a raised terrace overlooking the sea on Stegna Beach.

✉ Stegna Beach, Stegna, Northern Rhodes ☎ 22440 22632

Mavrikos (€€–€€€)

On a whitewashed terrace just outside the town walls, affording great views down onto the bay. Expect classic Greek meat and seafood dishes, including some delicious stews.

✉ Main Square, Lindos, Southern Rhodes ☎ 22440 31232

Mike's (€)

Good fish restaurant, tucked away down an alley running parallel to Sokratous Street and reached along a lane directly opposite Alexis Taverna.

✉ Off Sokratous, Rhodes Old Town ☎ 22410 23844

Philosophia Beach Taverna (€€–€€€)

A romantic spot overlooking the sea. Greek and international dishes are prepared using homegrown vegetables. Occasionally hosts wedding celebrations.

✉ Pefkos main beach, Southern Rhodes ☎ 22440 48044; www.philosophia-pefkos.com

Skala (€)

This laid-back taverna has tables set out on a terrace by the beach, and serves Greek fare with a weekly barbecue. Sunbeds and parasols are for hire by the waters' edge.

✉ Lindos Beach Road, Southern Rhodes
☎ 22440 31346

Best boat trips

Various small private companies offer one or several of these trips, departing on a daily basis through the high season, with slightly less regular departures through the low season. The best way to find out about the trips on offer on any given day is to walk down to the harbourfront, where each company has an information kiosk in front of its respective boats.

Rhodes Town to Lindos
Daily excursion boats run down the coast (journey time 2 hours) stopping in a bay for a swim on the way, with lunch in Lindos and time to visit the hilltop Acropolis.

Lindos to Pefkos
Take a ride in a glass-bottom boat to see underwater life – fish, sponges and sea urchins – with time for a swim in the crystal-clear turquoise water.

Rhodes Town to Faliraki

Offered as a sunset cruise, this trip along the east coast to Kalithea and Faliraki, with live music on board, makes for a romantic way to start the evening.

Rhodes Town to Symi

Many people's favourite, this trip includes Symi's harbour, overlooked by neoclassic mansions built by wealthy sponge merchants, plus a stop at Panormitis Monastery before heading home.

Rhodes Town to Chalki

Escape the crowds with a trip to this tiny island which has a year-round population of just 313. Expect tranquillity, tumbledown old stone cottages and several peaceful coves for bathing.

Rhodes Town to Nissiros

This small island is actually a dormant volcano (most recently active in 1933), where you can take a look in the crater exuding hot sulphuric gases.

Rhodes Town to Kos

Join an organized day-trip by high-speed catamaran (journey time 2 hours) to see Kos Town, home to an imposing Castle of the Knights of St John, Greek and Roman ruins and Ottoman-era minarets.

Rhodes Town to Marmaris

This popular, one-day, organized excursion gives visitors a chance to see Turkey, shop in the bustling bazaar and visit Marmaris Castle above the harbour. Take your passport with you.

Top beaches

Afandou for lots of space (➤ 104).

Fourni for a sense of really being away from
the rest of Rhodes and for the
spectacular backdrop of
forested mountains (➤ 48).

Glystra for superb sand, shallow water and absence of development (► 133).

Haraki for the convenience of the beachside promenade, or nearby Agia Agathi for simplicity and for excellent sand (► 109).

Pefkos for a selection of small beaches with good sand (► 143).

Plimiri for remoteness and space (► 144).

Prasonisi for wide open spaces and a choice of spots for windsurfing or sunbathing (► 145).

Traganou for clear water and white shingle (► 104).

Tsambika for absence of beachside development and wild surroundings (► 125).

Vlicha for a sense of luxury and good facilities (► 149).

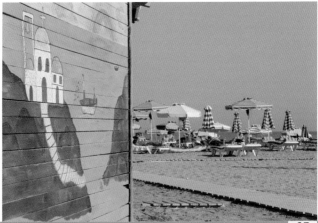

Stunning views

- Feraklos castle, Haraki (➤ 109)

- Ialyssos, from the fortress and cross (➤ 42–43)

- Kastrou Monolithos (➤ 48–49)

- Kritinia Kastellos (➤ 113)

- Lindos Acropolis (➤ 36–37)

- Monte Smith (➤ 83)

- Old Town walls, Rhodes (➤ 90–91)

- Profitis Ilias ridge (➤ 54–55)

- Roloi, the Turkish clock tower, Old Town (➤ 91)

- Tsambika monastery (➤ 125)

Top sports and activities

BOWLING
Strike Bowling
This eight-lane bowling alley just outside Kremasti has Internet access, pool tables, video games and a cafe.
✉ Eleftherias Avenue, Kremasti ☎ 22410 98233; www.strikebowlingclub.gr 🕐 10am–2am

BUNGEE JUMPING
New World Extreme Sports Company
At Faliraki the big orange towers of the bungee-jumping, sky-surfing, shriek-and-scream machine dominate the skyline. Billed as 45m of "sheer terror".
✉ The Crane, Faliraki Beach

CYCLING
Bicycle Centre
A range of bicycles, motorbikes and scooters for hire.
✉ 39 Griva, Rhodes New Town ☎ 22410 28315 🕐 8:30–7

Motoride
Scooters, quads and bicycles for rent.
✉ Faliraki ☎ 22410 86979; www.motoride-faliraki.com

GOLF
Afandou Golf Course
An 18-hole course of international standard; par 72. Clubs and pull cars are available for rent; lessons.
✉ Afandou ☎ 22410 51451; www.afandougolfcourse.com

TENNIS
Rhodes Tennis Club
Tennis may seem little too vigorous in the heat, but sea breezes will help you to keep cool.
✉ 4 N Sava, Elli Beach, Rhodes New Town ☎ 22410 25705

WATERSPORTS

Charlie's Water Sport Center

Right on Faliraki beach by the blue Sea Hotel, Charlie's
has water-skiing, banana boats, paragliding and all the
other popular activities.

✉ Faliraki beach ☎ 69326 50043 ⓒ May–Oct

Dive Med

Based on a handsome old *caique* moored at Mandraki
main road quay and offering trips along the coast to
permitted diving areas such as Thermes Kalithea.
Diving around the island shoreline is tightly controlled.

✉ Mandraki Harbour ☎ 22410 61115;
www.divemedcollege.com

Prasonisi Windsurfing

Great venue for windsurfing and the spectacular
and fast developing sport of kite-surfing. Instruction
is available.

✉ Prasonisi Beach ☎ 22410 91044; www.prasonisicenter.com

Pro Surf Center Blue Horizon

Behind the Blue Horizon Hotel at Ialyssos beach, this
wind surfing centre caters for beginners to experienced
surfers, including children. Expert tuition.

✉ Ialyssos beach ☎ 22410 95819; www.procenter-rhodes.com

Waterhoppers Diving Schools

Trips and dive training courses with experienced,
qualified instructors. One-day introductory courses to
more adventurous trips for the experienced. Operates
from own boat. Family packages also available.

✉ 45 Kritika Street, Rhodes New Town ☎ 22410 38146;
www.waterhoppers.com

Places to take the children

Archaeological sites

Fortunately the archaeological sites on Rhodes are fairly small compared to others elsewhere, which gives parents the chance to appreciate them without the children getting bored too quickly. None of the sites is very far from a beach, either, as a reward.

Faliraki Water Park

This huge complex is a major attraction. Family fun, with mega waterslides, aqua gym, wave pool and numerous food outlets.
✉ Faliraki (north end) ☎ 22410 84403; www.water-park.gr

Kadmos Riding Club

With stables for 35 horses and a sand arena, Kadmos offers private and group tuition for riders of all ages and levels, plus guided trekking through the surrounding woods and mountains.
✉ Asgourou (5km/3 miles inland from Ialyssos) ☎ 22410 96651; www.rhodesriding.com

Lardos Go-Karts

In Lardos village in the southeastern part of the island,

this great little go-kart track also has a cafe where parents can watch their children hurtle round the track.

✉ Lardos ☎ 22440 44510 ⏰ Daily in season 9:30am–late

Rhodes Aquarium

At the northern end of Rhodes Town, on the northern tip of the island, this combination of Aquarium and Research centre (► 79) attracts 200,000 visitors a year. It's an entertaining and educational mix of live exhibits such as turtles, whales and dolphins and display panels, explaining the fascinating underwater world around Rhodes.

✉ Rhodes Town ☎ 22410 27308 ⏰ Daily 9–8:30 (closes 4:30 in winter) 👤 Moderate

Stegna Beach

Avoid the crowds in Faliraki and Lindos, and head for Stegna Beach (► 115) on the east coast, near Archangelos. Backed by rocky cliffs, this low-key sand-and-pebble beach is perfect for the little ones.

Watersports

There are watersports facilities all around the island (► 67).

a drive around northern Rhodes

This route shows the contrast between the holiday coasts of northern Rhodes and the island's mountainous interior.

Leave Rhodes Town by the west coast road and pass through Ixia, Ialyssos and Kremasti. After 27km (17 miles) you reach Kalavarda and turn left, signed Salakos and Emponas. Climb steadily to Salakos then continue below the craggy, pine-clad slopes of Profitis Ilias (▶ 54–55).

At a junction by a tiny church, go left, signed Profitis Ilias and Eleoussa. Follow the twisting road uphill to reach Profitis Ilias.

Below the roadside *kafenío* is an Italian-era hotel and the Church of Profitis Ilias.

Leave Profitis Ilias by keeping straight ahead at the junction just beyond the cafe. Follow occasional signs for Archipoli and Eleoussa. Watch out for possible rough spots in the road. Keep left at first junction, signed Monastery Fountoukli and Eleoussa. Pass the wayside church of Agios Nikolaos Fountoukli and continue to Eleoussa.

Eleoussa was colonized by Italians in the early 20th century and their legacy is an art deco fountain at the village entrance, a square of old Italianate buildings, and a church.

Turn immediately right at the square, pass in front of the church steps, then go left at the junction and follow signs to reach Archipoli. Continue to the east coast road, passing on the way the monastery church of Agios Nektarios and the entrance road to Epta Piges (▶ 106–107). At the coast road, turn left for Rhodes Town.

You can divert to Kolimbia (▶ 111) or Afandou (▶ 104) beaches for a late dip on the way.

Distance 93km (58 miles)
Time 5–6 hours, depending on diversions to beaches
Start/end point Rhodes Town ✚ M24
Lunch Profitis Ilias *kafenío* (€)

Exploring

Rhodes Town is a captivating mix of the old and the new. Buried beneath today's modern town are the roots of an ancient Greek city, its classical elegance lost forever. Yet a sense of the past is everywhere. The surviving Old Town has weathered earthquake and bombardment and the wear and tear of time. Many parts have been heavily restored, but the main area is a fascinating mix of old buildings that reflect the history of the town from the classical and Byzantine periods to the medieval eras. The port area, too, reflects the island's ancient links to the sea, from the quaint fishing boats docked alongside the commercial harbour to the cruise ships and excursion boats sailing in and out of Mandraki. By contrast, Rhodes New Town shows the influence of Italian monumental building and the art deco style of the 1930s, while the main commercial district is a lively modern precinct.

Rhodes Town

Poli tis
Rodou
(Rhodes
Town)

Rhodes Town (Poli tis Rodou) can keep you busy for days. It is the duality of the place that makes it so compelling: the fascinating contrast of the Old Town with the emphatically modern New Town. The defensive walls that the Knights of St John built on a monumental scale ensured the Old Town's survival as a distinctive enclave compared with the changing world outside.

As soon as you enter the Old Town through any of the handsome gates that punctuate its walls, you feel the difference. Within lie museums and galleries, and a huge variety of cafes, tavernas and restaurants, all within the framework of a medieval city. The harbours were the key to the success of ancient Rhodes, and today they are a link between the old and the new. At Mandraki, with its old windmills and lines of expensive motor cruisers, yachts and colourful local ferries, you enter modern Rhodes, a world of frantic traffic along the harbourside Eleftherias Street. However, the pedestrianized quayside also means that you can relax and

watch the world sail by, while just across the way is the bustling New Market and behind it the busy heart of the New Town. Here you will find, alongside fashion shops, mouthwatering delicatessens and relaxed cafe terraces.

✚ M24 🚌 Town buses from opposite entrance to New Market (Nea Agora) 🚢 Excursion boats leave from Mandraki Harbour; inter-island ferries from Commercial Harbour
ℹ️ Greek National Tourist Organization, corner of Makariou/Papagou streets; City of Rhodes Tourist Information, Rimini Square; seasonal openings

ANAKTORO TON ARKHONTON (PALACE OF THE GRAND MASTERS)

Best places to see, ➤ 38–39.

Ancient Rhodes Exhibition

This is an outstanding collection of artefacts within the Palace of the Grand Masters that leads you through a series of displays from the Stone Age settlement of Rhodes through the classical to the Roman period. Among the many exhibits is a fine head of the Sun God Helios, Rhodes' mythic founder. A mosaic floor of the Middle Hellenistic period displays a superb "New Comedy Mask" that you would swear was a painting rather than an intricate mosaic. Look out for the little bronze figures of bulls and grasshoppers. There are splendid collections of pottery and household goods from all periods displayed in an imaginative way.

Medieval Exhibition

The Medieval Exhibition is housed in wings of the Palace of the Grand Masters and gives a vivid insight into the Byzantine, medieval and Turkish periods of Rhodes' long history. The commercial and trading history of the Byzantine period is well illustrated and there are fascinating depictions of how the town has developed, and indeed contracted, since its Hellenistic inception. Other exhibits portray the life and times of the Knights of St John and there are displays of manuscripts and icons.

✚ *Rhodes Town d5* ✉ Palace of the Grand Masters, Kleovoulou Square, Old Town ☎ 22410 62570 ◷ Apr–Oct Tue–Sun 8–8, Mon 12–7; Nov–Mar Tue–Sun 8:30–3 ✋ Expensive ▯ Cafe inside Palace (€€) ❷ 2,400 Years Exhibition

ASTIKI PINAKOTHIKI (MUNICIPAL ART GALLERY)

Rhodes is the proud guardian of one of the finest collections of modern Greek art in existence. The collections are housed in separate galleries. Two are in the Old Town; the Municipal Art

Gallery, which contains a collection of fine engravings, while the second, the smaller **Centre of Contemporary Art,** exhibits and promotes work by contemporary artists. The third building, Nestoridion Melathron, is in the New Town (➤ 78).

The main collection of the Municipal Art Gallery is housed in the upper level of an attractive medieval-style building and contains one of the finest collections of modern Greek art in existence. The gallery was founded in 1962 by Andreas Ioannou, the then Prefect of the Dodecanese. The collection, not all of which is on show at any one time, covers various periods from 1863 to the 1940s and gives a rich insight to the development of modern Greek painting.

www.mgamuseum.gr

✚ *Rhodes Town e5* ✉ 2 Symis Square, Old Town ☎ 22410 23766
🕐 Tue–Fri 9–3, 6–9, Sat 10–12 ✋ Moderate (ticket covers all three venues)
🍴 Evdimou (€)

Centre of Contemporary Art

✉ 179 Sokratous Street, Old Town ☎ 22410 36646 🕐 Tue–Sat 8–2
✋ Moderate 🍴 Cafe next door (€–€€)

Nestoridion Melathron

The splendid Nestoridion Melathron, housed in the one-time Olympic Hotel at the heart of New Town's hotel district is arguably the gem in the trio of galleries. The building has been thoroughly modernized and contains superb collections from the 1860s to the present day. The displays include an extensive number of paintings and prints, together with sculptures and drawings by celebrated Greek artists.

✉ 1 Haritou Square ☎ 22410 43780
🕐 Tue–Fri 9–2, Sat 10–12
♿ Moderate 🍴 Cafe (€–€€)

DHIMOTIKA LOUTRA (MUNICIPAL BATHS)

The *hammam*, or Turkish bath, is the most tangible legacy of nearly 300 years of Turkish influence on Rhodes. Known officially as the Municipal Baths, the much renovated *hammam* is a rare example of a working Turkish bath in Greece. The exterior of the building is unremarkable, but inside are all the hallmarks of Moorish hydromechanics: underfloor pipes that carry the water which is heated by olive wood fires; side chambers with wash sinks and marble floor slabs; and the star-pierced dome above the central hot room. There are separate areas for men and women, as bathers are naked. For an extra charge you can lie on a marble slab and enjoy a vigorous soaping, massage and exfoliation session. Wooden slippers are supplied but bring your own towel.

✚ *Rhodes Town d7* ✉ Arionos Square, Old Town ☎ 22410 27739 🕐 Mon–Fri 10–5, Sat 8–5 ✋ Moderate 🍴 To Diafani, Arionos Square (€) ❓ No photography allowed

ENYDREIO (AQUARIUM)

The Italian-era Aquarium stands in a breezy location on Ammos Point at the most northerly tip of Rhodes Town. This building is a monument to 1930s art deco, right down to the sea horse and seashell reliefs on the doorcase. The building is an outstation of the Greek National Centre for Marine Research and a great deal of research work is carried out. The Aquarium was renovated in 2001. It is housed in the basement of the building and contains a number of sea-fed tanks displaying various Aegean species of fish, mammals and marine organisms including sea turtles.

✚ *Rhodes Town c1* ✉ Kos Street ☎ 22410 27308 🕐 Daily 9–8:30 (closes 4:30 in winter) ✋ Moderate 🍴 Cafes at Elli Beach (€–€€)

EVRAIKIS SINIKIAS
(OLD JEWISH QUARTER)

The Old Jewish Quarter is contained
within the most easterly section of
Rhodes Old Town, where Jewish
merchants and artisans were permitted to live during the Turkish
occupation of the island. The focus of the area is Platia Martyron
Evraion, the Square of the Jewish Martyrs, from where an
estimated 1,604 Rhodian Jews were deported to concentration
camps by Nazi forces in 1943. A simple tree-shaded monument
records the fact in several languages. The square has a charming
sea horse fountain and is flanked on one side by a 15th-century
Archbishop's Palace. A short way along Pindharou to the east, a
right turn leads down Dosiadou Street and into Simiou Street,
where stands a surviving **synagogue,** itself a reconstruction by
the Knights after the original was destroyed during the first Great
Turkish siege. Most of the Old Jewish Quarter is a major tourist
attraction, its main streets and squares crammed with gift shops,
cafes and restaurants. All roads lead to the crowded shopping
street of Sokratous, via Ippokratous Square. Intriguing narrow
alleyways lead off the main squares.

🚪 *Rhodes Town f7* ✉ Rhodes Old Town 🍴 Numerous cafes and
restaurants in Platia Martyron Evraion (€€–€€€)

Jewish Synagogue

✉ Dosiadou/Simiou streets 🕐 Daily mornings only (may be closed
during winter months) 💰 Donations welcome

IPPOTON (STREET OF THE KNIGHTS)

Best places to see, ➤ 44–45.

LIMANI MANDRAKIOU (MANDRAKI HARBOUR)

The attractive Mandraki Harbour is the most northerly of Rhodes'
three harbours and by far the most interesting. This was the
ancient "sheep pen", the name in Greek being *mandri*, a name

often used for small, encircling harbours. Mandraki was one of the five ports of ancient Rhodes. It was the naval port and was known as the "small harbour" as opposed to the "great harbour", the present Commercial Harbour. The entrance to ancient Mandraki could be sealed with chains. Legend claims that the harbour entrance was spanned by the legendary Colossus of Rhodes, but there is no proof of this. Today twin columns bearing statues of Rhodian deer, a stag and doe, stand on either side of the harbour gap. A row of restored medieval windmills, symbols of the days when corn was ground at the harbourside, stands along the outer quay. At the seaward end of the quay is the fortress of St Nicholas, built in the 1460s and now the site of a lighthouse. On its landward side the harbour is bordered by the busy Eleftherias Street, at the end of which is Platia Vasileos Georgiou I. Here the Italians left a collection of interesting monumental buildings in a mix of Venetian, Gothic and Ottoman architectural styles. On the quayside stands the Ekklisia Evangelismou, the Cathedral of St John the Evangelist.

✚ *Rhodes Town d4* ✉ New Town 🍴 Akteon Café (€€), Eleftherias Square

MESEONIKI TAFROS RODOU (OLD TOWN MOAT)

The Old Town Moat was always dry, but was still a formidable barrier to attack. Now landscaped and dotted with palm trees and pines, it is a delightful place in which to stroll. There are several entry points to the moat, but a logical approach is through Pyli Petru, the Gate of St Peter, reached from Alexandrias Square at the south end of Mandraki Harbour, and opposite the southern wall of the New Market. The way passes between towering walls and soon reaches a widening of the moat at Exit 1, the handsome Pyli Ambouaz, the d'Amboise Gate. In the bed of the moat lie the remains of a medieval quarry. Soon you come to a central earthwork. Keep to its right. The track leads beneath a bridge, then comes to another earthwork where old stone mortar balls litter the ground like giant hailstones. Keep to the right again. The track passes beneath another bridge, widens again at the Melina Mercouri Open Air Theatre then exits onto the harbour front road called Prometheus.

✚ *Rhodes Town c6* ✉ Old Town
🍴 New Market and Gate of St Peter
(€–€€) ❓ Concerts and shows are held at the Melina Mercouri Theatre in summer

MONTE SMITH

The name Monte Smith (after the British admiral Sydney Smith) has usurped the Greek name for the 112m (367ft) hill that overlooks Rhodes Town. The hilltop was the religious and ceremonial focus of the magnificent 5th-century BC city of Rhodes that fanned out in geometrical elegance below its eastern escarpment. On the summit stood temples and monuments, but earthquakes and subsequent neglect did much to efface all their architectural glory. The Italians partially restored a 3rd-century BC Temple of Apollo, of which only a cluster of columns survives. At the bottom of the escarpment is an Italian restoration of a theatre and stadium that retain just a few original fragments.

✚ *Rhodes Town a8* ✉ 2km (1.2 miles) west of New Town ⏱ Open access 🚌 No 5 bus to Agios Ioannis, every 40 mins from opposite New Market entrance

MOUSEIO ARCHAIOLOGIKO (ARCHAEOLOGICAL MUSEUM)

Rhodes' Archaeological Museum is located in the old Hospital of the Knights, a rather severe, but impressive, 15th-century Gothic building. A steep staircase leads to the magnificent infirmary hall with its central colonnade, the capitals of which are carved with heraldic devices. The smaller side chambers of the upper gallery contain some fine artefacts including the celebrated, yet unglamorous, Marine Venus, a sea-eroded 4th-century BC statue of Aphrodite, that inspired the novelist Lawrence Durrell. In other chambers are superb Rhodian amphorae, some fine Attic pottery pieces, and Mycenaean jewellery. Look for the 4th-century gravestone of Kalliarista and its touching epigram inscribed by her husband, as well as the tiny vases and bowls that formed a child's funerary gifts. Beyond the upper gallery is a sunlit sculpture garden.

✚ *Rhodes Town d6* ✉ Mousiou Square, Old Town
☎ 22410 65256 🕐 Mon 12:30–7, Tue–Sun 8–2:30
♿ Expensive 🍴 Cafes in Ermou Street (€€)

MOUSEIO TIS KOSMIKIS TECHNIS (MUSEUM OF DECORATIVE ARTS)

The Museum of Decorative Arts is housed in a ground floor room that was once part of the armoury of the Knights of St John. It is more of a folk art museum than its name implies, and has a charming and colourful collection of domestic goods from the 16th to the early 20th century. These include folk costumes from the islands of Symi and Astypalaea, carved and painted chests and bedsteads, carved wall cupboards and other furnishings. There is a large collection of ceramics and fabrics, including carpets and such distinctive items as embroidered bed tents.

✚ *Rhodes Town d6* ✉ Argyrokastrou Square, Old Town ☎ 22410 65246
🕐 Tue–Sun 8:30–2:30 ✋ Inexpensive 🍴 Cafes in Ermou Street (€€)

MOUSEIO VIZANTINO (BYZANTINE MUSEUM)

The Byzantine Museum is housed in the splendid Church of
Panagia Kastrou, the Virgin of the Castle. This 11th-century building
has had a remarkable history. Originally it was the Byzantine
Cathedral of Rhodes and had a classic Byzantine "cross-in-square"
form, with a central dome. The church was converted to a Roman
Catholic cathedral by the Knights of St John, who replaced the
dome with a barrel vault and cross vaults. During the Turkish
occupation of Rhodes the building was converted into a mosque
complete with minaret, removed during the Italian reconstruction.
Today, the church contains a few Byzantine and post-Byzantine
icons and wall paintings, sculptures and mosaic fragments.

➕ *Rhodes Town e6* ✉ Mousiou Square, Old Town 🕐 Apr–Oct Tue–Sun 9–3
🍽 Inexpensive 🍴 Cafes in Ermou Street (€€)

NEA POLI (NEW TOWN)

The New Town is an appealing and cosmopolitan place, a mix of Italian-era art deco and municipal buildings, bland modern hotels, a sprinkling of 1930s mansions, and the shops and offices of the commercial centre.

On the Mandraki waterfront, the Italian-built Nea Agora, the New Market, is a striking feature. Its Ottoman-inspired entrance arch leads to a heptagonal courtyard that is lined with shops, food kiosks, cafes and tavernas, and has a fish market at its centre. The bustle of the New Market has ebbed in recent years, but there are still plenty of shops and stalls. The exterior perimeter of the building, on Plateia Rimini, has a marvellous selection of delicatessens, bakeries and open-fronted shops selling spices, herbs, nuts, liquor, sweets and Greek specialities. The seafront perimeter is lined with cafes and wickedly indulgent *zaharoplastios* (cafe-patisseries). Northwest of the market is busy Kiprou Square, the hub of Rhodes' shopping district. The New Town has pleasant green areas such as the Municipal Park, reached from El Venizelou Street, and the Municipal Gardens, reached from Rimini Square.

✚ *Rhodes Town d5* 🍴 Bistrot 46 (€; ➤ 94), Kontiki (€€; ➤ 95)

a walk around the Old Town

This short walk through the medieval Old Town gives some idea of the pleasure that can be had from seeking out the more remote quarters of this fascinating area.

Go through Pyli Panagias (St Mary's Gate), cross Rodiou, then cross the courtyard of the ruined Church of Our Lady of the City. Keep straight ahead along a paved walkway (Alhadef) fringed with trees. Just before the arch of the Agandia Gate, turn right, up Dionissiou (watch for traffic) and continue along Ekatonos. Pass the ruins of a Roman building, then bear second right along the narrow Tlipolemou.

The characteristic narrow alleyways of the Old Town, with their *hokhláki* (pebble mosaic surfacing), begin to appear.

Where the lane divides, take the right-hand branch (still Tlipolemou), pass beneath an arch, cross Perikleous, then go under another arch to reach the square of Panagiotu Rodiu and the Church of Agia Triada. Pass in front of the church then go left along the twisting Laokoontos to reach a T-junction. Here turn left along Praxitelous, then go right along Kimonous, then left along Klisthenous.

These tiny alleyways are the heart and soul of the Old Town.

At a T-junction turn right along Archbishop Efthymiou and keep round right to reach a small square. Turn left along Omirou. After about 100m (110yds) go right through an arched opening into Dorieos Square.

In the square is the impressive Tzami Rejep Pascha
(► 92), and the three-aisled basilica of Agios Fanouriou.

*Leave the square by the far left-hand corner, then turn
right along the wonderful Agios Fanouriou
and follow it to its end to the busy
shopping street of Sokratous.*

Distance 1.5km (1 mile)
Time 1 hour
Start point St Mary's Gate, Commercial Harbour
(next gate north of Marine Gate) ✚ *Rhodes
Town f6*
End point Sokratous ✚ *Rhodes Town d6*
Lunch The Walk Inn, Dorieos Square (€)
Church of Agia Triada 🕐 Tue–Sun 8–2:30

PALIA POLI (OLD TOWN)

Best places to see, ➤ 50–51.

PARALIA TIS 'ELLIS (ELLI BEACH)

Beaches of variable quality lie to either side of the most northerly tip of Rhodes' New Town. The long, west-facing beach is backed by a busy ring road and it can be very windy. It's certainly considered better for windsurfing than as a good place for sunbathing. The more sheltered Elli Beach on the eastern side of the headland is a long crescent of shingle that sets off the banks of luxury hotels dominating the shoreline. Crowds of sunbathers are the price of Elli being a town beach and it gets very busy in peak season. All types of beach furniture and watersports are available.

✚ *Rhodes Town c2* ✉ Kos Street ▮ Cafes and snack bars along beachfront (€–€€)

TIHI TIS POLIS (OLD TOWN WALLS)

Rhodes' Old Town is defined dramatically by its 4km (2.5 miles) of defensive walls, their silent precincts haunted by the ghosts of bloody siege and ferocious assault. The present walls owe their monumental form to the fortress mentality of the Knights of St John. Major expansion of the walls came in the 1450s as threats of Turkish invasion galvanized the Knights into improving their defences. The first Turkish siege of 1480 was repulsed, but continuing fears of invasion saw even greater expansion of the walls. The dry moat (➤ 82) was deepened and made wider, powerful bastions were erected at strategic points, and island-like earthworks were erected within the moat to create extra defences and to form bottleneck traps for attackers. All of these features survive, partially restored and redesigned in places by the Italians, but generally true to the originals. The walls are still being refurbished today. Walking the walls on organized tours between the Palace of the Grand Masters (► 38–39) and the Koskinou Gate gives an airy view of the stark outer world of siege and defence, as well as marvellous glimpses of the jumbled inner city with its skyline of Byzantine tiled roofs, slender minarets, palm trees and orchards, its dusty backyards and gardens, serpentine alleyways and crumbling walls.

✚ *Rhodes Town d8* 🕓 Tue–Sun 8:30–1. Tickets from Palace of the Grand Masters, admissions desk 💷 Inexpensive ❓ The inner edge and outer openings of the walls are unguarded; exercise care, especially with children

TZAMI SOULEIMAN AND TZAMI TOU MOURAD REIS

Ottoman buildings on Rhodes have tended to suffer neglect since the Turks were ousted from the island in 1912. However, sporadic refurbishment of Turkish buildings does take place, and the sizeable Muslim population on Rhodes ensures continuing use of several historic mosques. There is no Turkish Quarter as such, but there are a number of splendid old mosques scattered throughout the Old Town. Finest of these is **Tzami Souleiman** (Süleyman Mosque), erected by the Turkish conqueror of Rhodes in 1522 as a thanksgiving for his triumph. Its rose-red walls and shallow dome dominate the top end of Sokratous. Close by, on Orfeos, is the Roloi (Turkish clock tower).

At the northern end of the New Town is **Tzami Tou Mourad Reis** (Murad Reis Mosque), located within an engagingly unkempt and

tree-shaded Muslim cemetery. The entrance courtyard has *hokhláki* (pebble mosaic) flooring and in one corner stands the little circular mausoleum of Mourad Reis, a commander of the Turkish navy during the 1522 siege of Rhodes. The cemetery has its own little forest of slender gravestones; the male memorials crowned with turbans, the female memorials, simple blades of stone. There are a number of domed tombs one containing the remains of a Shah of Persia. At the northern end of the graveyard is the Villa Cleobolus, once home to the novelist Lawrence Durrell and now renovated as a small museum-cum-gallery.

Other notable buildings are **Tzami Rejep Pascha** (Retzep Pasha Mosque) and the impressive **Tzami Sultan Mustafa** (Mustafa Pasha Mosque).

Tzami Souleiman
✚ *Rhodes Town d6* ✉ Sokratous Square, Old Town 🕐 Not open to public 🍴 Cafes in Orfeos and Sokratous (€–€€)

Tzami Tou Mourad Reis
✚ *Rhodes Town d3* ✉ Koundouriotou Square 🕐 9–6 (variable) ✋ Free (small donation appreciated if caretaker present) 🍴 Cavalliere, Ioannou Kazouli Street (➤ 94–95)

Tzami Rejep Pascha
✚ *Rhodes Town d7* ✉ Dorieos Square, Old Town 🕐 Not open to public 🍴 Cafes in square (€)

Tzami Sultan Mustafa
✚ *Rhodes Town d7* ✉ Arionos Square, Old Town 🕐 Not open to public 🍴 Cafes in square (€)

HOTELS

Best Western Plaza Hotel (€€€)
Top-of-the-range hotel with comfortable rooms and swimming pool, lying between Elli beach and the medieval walls. The breakfast buffet is outstanding.

✉ Ierou Lochou 7, New Town ☎ 22410 22501; www.rhodesplazahotel.com

Domus Studios Hotel (€€)
A renovated old building providing four chic studios with wooden beamed ceilings, exposed stonework and modern interiors.

✉ Apolonion 11, Old Town ☎ 22410 25965; www.domus-studios-rhodes.gr

Hotel Anastasia (€)
A pleasant, family-run hotel with character. Located in leafy garden area off main street. Straightforward high-ceilinged rooms. Outside breakfast area beneath a hibiscus canopy.

✉ 28 Oktovriou 46, New Town ☎ 22410 28007; www.anastasia-hotel.com

Hotel Attiki (€)
Renovated in spring 2009, this friendly, welcoming hotel has 10 stylish rooms, a pretty courtyard garden with orange trees and potted geraniums. Breakfast is served on the roof terrace.

✉ Theofiliskous and Haritos 2, Old Town ☎ 22410 36596; www.hotelattiki.com 🕙 Closed Dec–Feb

Hotel Spot (€€)
Small and friendly hotel that is in a handy, but quiet location at the heart of Rhodes Old Town. Buffet breakfast included.

✉ Perikleous 21, Old Town ☎ 22410 34737; www.spothotelrhodes.gr 🕙 Closed Nov–late Mar

Marco Polo Mansions (€€–€€€)
For the ultimate Old Town experience, this splendid 15th-century building in the old Turkish Quarter is the place for style and flair, with surviving Ottoman features adding to the ambience.

✉ Agios Fanouriou 42, Old Town ☎ 22410 25562; www.marcopolomansion.gr

Pension Minos (€)

A big roof terrace with superb views over Old Town is a bonus at this reasonable option in a quiet area. Breakfast is extra.

✉ Omirou 5, Old Town ☎ 22410 31813; www.minospension.com

Pink Elephant (€)

Tucked away in a quiet square with lots of cosy charm, this small, friendly pension has pleasant rooms round a small courtyard.

✉ Timikida 9, Old Town ☎ 22410 22469; www.pinkelephantpension.com

Spirit of the Knights Boutique Hotel (€€€)

In a carefully restored medieval building, this family-run boutique hotel has six romantic suites (some with private *hammam*). Breakfast is served in the garden, complete with a fountain, sun beds and an outdoor jacuzzi

✉ Alexandridou 14, Old Town ☎ 22410 39765; www.rhodesluxuryhotel.com

RESTAURANTS

Alexis Taverna (€€€)

See page 58.

Aspro Piato (€€)

Opened in spring 2009, this chic minimalist restaurant serves refined Greek cuisine at reasonable prices. Locals recommend it for its succulent grilled steaks and excellent wine list.

✉ G Griva, New Town ☎ 22410 77925 🕐 Varies according to season

Bistrot 46 (€)

Busy, popular cafe-bar in New Town's liveliest street. Serves good snacks and has a huge range of hot and cold drinks from coffee to beers, wines and spirits.

✉ Amerikis 46b, New Town ☎ 22410 78369; www.bistrot46.gr
🕐 Lunch, dinner

Cavalliere (€)

Classy *gelateria* (ice cream parlour) and patisserie serving a large range of home-made ice cream, pastries and cake. They also serve pizza and other snacks and have a good wine and liquor list in this comfortable cafe with free WiFi.

✉ Ioannou Kazouli, New Town ☎ 22410 22932 ◷ All day

Ellinikon (€€–€€€)

This popular restaurant has the added bonus of a pleasant garden terrace. There are tasty appetizers and salads, and plenty of meat and fish dishes.

✉ Papanikolaou 6, New Town ☎ 22410 28111 ◷ 6pm–1am

Hatzikelis (€€–€€€)

There's a great Greek atmosphere in this friendly restaurant. Excellent fish dishes, good *mezédhes* (starters) and meat dishes, made using the freshest local produce.

✉ Alhadef 9, Old Town ☎ 22410 27215 ◷ Lunch, dinner

Island Lipsi Restaurant (€€)

In a big medieval dining room with exposed stone walls and wooden beamed ceilings, this friendly restaurant offers a wide selection of traditional Greek dishes such as *kleftiko* (baked lamb with feta cheese and potatoes) and *gemista* (stuffed tomatoes with rice), plus pizza and pasta.

✉ Agisandrou 18, Old Town ☎ 22410 33903; www.restaurantlipsi.com ◷ Varies according to season

Kontiki (€€)

Opened in 1967, the Kontiki is still going strong after 40 years and is hard to miss, floating in Mandraki Harbour. The cooking is excellent, predominantly Greek but with modern fusion influences, a much more interesting menu than it might first appear.

✉ Mandraki Harbour, New Town ☎ 22410 20302; http://kontiki.itgo.com ◷ Daily 6pm–midnight (bar/cafe opens 8am)

Marco Polo Café (€€)

Wonderful location in a romantic courtyard garden that measures the history of Rhodes Old Town from Byzantine times, through the era of the Knights to the Turkish period. Enjoy tasty *mezédhes*, delicious savoury pies and drinks in fine surroundings.

✉ Agios Fanouriou 40–42, Old Town ☎ 22410 29115 ⏰ All day

Mike's (€)

See page 59.

Myrovolos (€–€€)

Hidden away in a side street off Sokratous, this informal taverna is much loved by locals. Expect tasty dishes such as octopus, stuffed peppers and pork fillet, friendly waiters and occasional Greek music.

✉ Lachitos 13, Old Town ☎ 22410 38693 ⏰ Varies according to season

Nisiros (€€)

Standard fare in this big taverna-restaurant at the heart of the finest medieval street in the Old Town. Prices tend to be slightly atmospheric, to match the setting.

✉ Agios Fanouriou 45–47, Old Town ☎ 22410 31471 ⏰ Lunch, dinner

Pizanias (€€–€€€)

Known to locals as Pizanis (after the owner's surname), this excellent seafood eatery is officially called Sea Star. Fresh fish is cooked on a barbecue outside, and served at tables on a leafy square.

✉ Sofokleous 24, Old Town ☎ 22410 31884 ⏰ Varies according to season

Rodon Café (€€€)

There's smart service and international cuisine at this stylish restaurant in Rhodes' casino, with dancing to live music for afters.

✉ Georgiou Papanikolaou 4, New Town ☎ 22410 97500; www.casinorodos.gr ⏰ 8pm–2am

Romeo Taverna and Grill (€€)

Big menu of Greek and Eastern Mediterranean dishes at this long-established restaurant, located in old building off Sokratous Street. Good selection of *mezédhes* (starters) and main dishes.

Also has vegetarian options. Wine list features Rhodian Villaré as well as reasonable house wine. Live Greek music.

✉ Menekleous 7–9, Old Town ☎ 22410 25186; www.romeo.gr

🕐 All day. Last orders 1am

Sarris (€€)

For good service, spotless surroundings and a pretty location at the heart of the Old Town, this is a good bet. *Mezédhes* selection is good, there is an ever-changing wine selection and home-made soups are a speciality.

✉ Evdimou 18, Old Town ☎ 22410 73707; www.sarristavern.com 🕐 All day

Yiannis Taverna (€)

Popular, family-run taverna without frills, but with excellent food and drink and outstanding value. The friendly host Yiannis Balaskas and his staff never seem to stop, as they serve up classic Greek dishes with great courtesy.

✉ Platonos 41, off Sokratous Street, Old Town ☎ 22410 36535

🕐 10am–midnight

SHOPPING

ARTS AND CRAFTS

Astero

Escape from the deluge of souvenir shops in Sokratous Street and into the start of Fanouriou where you will find Michael Hatzis's shop selling superb, authentic antiques.

✉ Agios Fanouriou 4, Old Town ☎ 22410 34753

Kyriakos K Hartofilis

Hand-painted Byzantine icons for sale in this workshop outlet. The artist can be seen at work in the shop.

✉ Sokratous 81, Old Town ☎ 22410 22153

Museum Shop

Run by the Hellenic Ministry of Culture, this place has exhibitions and stylish pottery, sculpture, books, prints and postcards.

✉ Symis Square, Old Town ☎ 22410 76236

Marinos Wine Store
There's a huge selection of alcoholic drinks of all kinds at this long established business.
✉ Ermou 23, Old Town ☎ 22410 77141

Mike's Zaharaplasto
Delicious treats on offer, try *melekouni*, a sesame seed biscuit with honey, or *moshopougi*, a pastry filled with almonds and spice and covered with icing sugar. Also a big selection of ice creams.
✉ Sofokli Venizelou, New Town ☎ 22410 66510

Papadopoulos Liqueur Store
Going strong for more than 60 years, this New Market shop has a dazzling selection of spirits and liqueurs.
✉ Averof 42, New Market, New Town ☎ 22410 27485

GIFTS
Aelos
Some stylish pieces are on offer here; a good selection of painted wooden artefacts, ceramics and jewellery.
✉ Apellou 5, Old Town ☎ 22410 24203

Natura Greca
Natural cosmetics including mastiha products from Hios and Olive skin care products (made from olive oil).
✉ Sokratous 78–80, Old Town ☎ 22410 70067; www.naturagreca.com

JEWELLERY
E Karidis Jewellery
Good choice of gold and silver watches and jewellery.
✉ Ermou 61, Old Town ☎ 22410 20381

Lalaounis
Greece's top jewellery designer, Athens-based Lalaounis, crafts fine gold and silver pieces inspired by ancient techniques such as granulation and filigree.
✉ Mousiou Square, Old Town ☎ 22410 24793

MUSIC AND MEDIA
Manuel Music Center
This New Town shop has a terrific collection of CDs covering just about everything, including authentic Greek sounds.

✉ Amerikis 93, New Town ☎ 22410 28266

ENTERTAINMENT AND NIGHTLIFE

Bebe Music Bar
Formerly known as Mojo Bar, Bebe is known for its great music – predominately disco, 80s and house, with occasional guest DJs.

✉ Miltiadou 41, Old Town 🕓 May–Oct daily 8pm–3am; Nov–Apr Fri–Sat 10pm–3am

Besara
A bohemian-style cafe-bar staging occasional live jazz. Owned by an Australian lady, it's popular with locals and stays open all year.

✉ Sofokleous 11–13, Old Town ☎ 22410 30363 🕓 May–Oct daily 10am–3am; Nov–Apr Thu–Sun 5pm–3am

Casino Rhodos
A major entertainment venue with 300 slot machines and a gaming room with 30 tables offering American roulette, blackjack and Caribbean stud poker. Minimum gaming age is 23. Passport required. Fairly relaxed dress code, but no jeans or shorts.

✉ Hotel Grande Albergo delle Rosa, Georgiou Papanikolaou 4, New Town ☎ 22410 97500; www.casinorhodos.gr

Colorado Entertainment Centre
A three-in-one choice for the dedicated. Go to the Colorado Pub for full-on rock, the Colorado Club for techno, hip hop and R&B sounds, and the Heaven Bar for simply relaxing.

✉ Orfanidou and Akti Miaouli, New Town ☎ 22410 75120 🕓 May–Oct daily 11pm–5am

Greek Folk Dance Theatre
Greek folk dance performances with traditional costumes are staged during the season by the excellent Nelly Dimoglou Theatre

Company at this attractive venue. For anyone who wants to learn more, there are classes, seminars and workshops on offer after the show.

✉ Andronicou, Old Town (down lane on left of Municipal Baths) ☎ 22410 20157/29085 🕐 May–Oct Mon, Wed, Fri 9:20pm

Havana

On the go since 1998 and located on a street well known for its vast selection of bars, trendy Havana is one of the busiest in the area. It has a cosy wood-and-stone interior decorated with mirrors and candles, and plays a great selection of jazz, soul and R&B.

✉ Miltiadou 9, Old Town ☎ 694 4314 724 (mobile)

Rhodes Municipal Theatre

Stages an excellent programme of music, dance and theatre throughout the year, often featuring top performers. Well worth a visit even if you have little understanding of the Greek language. The music events especially can be superb. Details from tourist information centres (➤ 29).

✉ Vasileos Georgiou I Square, New Town ☎ 22410 30668

Sound and Light Show

Popular recorded show telling the story of the Turkish siege of the city in 1522. Multilingual performances on different evenings and at different times from Monday to Saturday during the season, in English, German, Swedish and French, with two performances in Greek. Check at tourist information centres for times of performances.

✉ Gardens of the Palace of the Grand Masters, off Rimini Square, Old Town ☎ Box Office 22410 21922

Viveur

A trendy little wine bar which plays a good mix of Greek and foreign music, with occasional guest DJs.

✉ Platonos 16 and Evripidou, Old Town ☎ 69372 28252 and 69422 88200; www.viveur.gr

Northern Rhodes

Symi

Alimnia

Afandou

The best beach life and nightlife are in the north of the island, at lively resorts such as Faliraki and Ixia. However, if you travel beyond to where the crowds thin out you discover an entirely different island, where rugged pine-clad mountains lie behind long stretches of empty beaches.

In the remote interior of Rhodes are quiet villages and hamlets, where time passes unnoticed and where Byzantine churches preserve an atmosphere of utter peace. You can also visit the island of Symi, one of the most beautiful little islands in Greece and an easy day trip from Rhodes Town.

AFANDOU

Afandou beach is entirely detached from the village of the same name. The beach runs for several kilometres along the rather scruffy, but refreshingly undeveloped foreshore of Afandou Bay and is backed by a flanking access road. There is usually room enough to breathe on the sand and shingle even at the height of the season, and there are watersports and beach equipment available in summer. At the north end of the main beach is Traganou Beach, all white shingle and translucent water in the shelter of Traganou Headland. At the north end of Traganou Beach, beyond a rocky bluff, is a small beach with caves in the cliff wall of the headland at its far end.

The village of Afandou is a classic example of a coastal community that initially migrated inland to escape the relentless pirate raids of the Byzantine period. The village's name is said to derive from the word for "hidden" or "invisible", neatly defining its origins. Today's Afandou is indeed invisible, even from the coast road, and is reached along several link roads that terminate at the

attractive village square with its canopied tavernas and cafes. The square is overlooked by Agios Loukas, the Church of the Assumption, which houses an interesting folklore exhibition.

✚ K20 ✉ East coast, 16km (10 miles) south of Rhodes Town 🍴 O Mimakos (€€) 🚌 East side bus, Rhodes–Afandou (Rimini Square) ❓ Pre-Lenten Carnival, seventh Sun before Easter

ARCHANGELOS

The large village of Archangelos stands amid a startling landscape of limestone cliffs and rocky hills. It is a bustling, down to earth place, the centre of an important farming area. The downside is that the main street has succumbed to the unrelenting racket of scooters and motorbikes. The Knights of St John had a castle here and its evocative, overgrown ruins are reached by going halfway along the left-hand branch of the main street. Turn left up a narrow alleyway then keep straight across a little square and go up Sarika Anastasi, following signs for the Acropolis. On the way down, visit the handsome church of Archangel Gabriel Patitiriotis. Clustered round the church is the older, quieter part of the village; quite distinctively Rhodian in its buildings and courteous residents.

✚ K18 ✉ East coast, 33km (20 miles) south of Rhodes Town
🍴 Savas (€; ➤ 128) 🚌 East side bus, Rhodes–Archangelos, daily (Rimini Square) ❓ Mid-Aug, week-long Cultural Festival; 8 Nov, Feast of the Archangels

EMBONAS

This large mountain village is the centre of the Rhodian wine trade. Here are located the island's vineyards on terraced fans that spill down from the stark slopes of 1,215m (3,986ft) Mount Attavyros. The Emery Winery, at the western outskirts of Embonas, stages conducted tours of its processing plant and caters for numerous coach parties. The village also does a good trade in carpet weaving, embroidery and general souvenirs. Take a stroll in the upper reaches of Embonas, where there are a number of venerable carpet weavers at work, especially near the Church of Panayia.

➕ D9 ✉ 58km (36 miles) southwest of Rhodes Town 🍴 Bakis Taverna (€; ► 58) 🚌 West side bus, Rhodes–Embonas, daily (Averof Street) ❓ Tours of Emery Winery, daily 9:30–3:30 or by appointment. Free ☎ 22410 29111; www.emery.gr

EPTA PIGES (THE SEVEN SPRINGS)

The sun-dappled enclave of Epta Piges was created by the Italians in the 1920s to supply water for irrigating the coastal colony of Kolimbia. The eponymous Seven Springs are hidden somewhere amid deep woodland. A narrow aqueduct-tunnel, 186m (610ft) long, siphons off water from just below the site car park to a pretty lake and waterfall hidden among the trees. Most guidebooks invite you to splash your way through this nightmare, but it is better to stay in the open air by walking directly uphill from the tunnel entrance to reach the access road and the halfway escape shaft. Cross the road and follow a landscaped path opposite (unsigned) to the holding dam where the tunnel disburses its water. The artificial lake is deep, non-potable and definitely not for diving into.

✚ K19 ✉ East coast, 30km (19 miles) south of Rhodes Town ⏰ Open access 🎫 Free 🍴 Seasonal taverna beside car park (€€) 🚌 East side bus, Rhodes–Kolimbia, daily (Rimini Square). Only to main road junction, then 4km (2.5 miles) to site

FALIRAKI

Rhodes's major beach resort of Faliraki is focused entirely on tourism, all of which is based on the sweep of sand that lines the long foreshore. The palatial hotels at the north end cater for a more restrained clientele than the youthful crowds who frequent the main resort, where every kind of watersport is available. It's generally harmless, non-stop party time in summer Faliraki, but over-the-top drunkenness, and some serious violence, have brought a crackdown by the authorities and the police that has incuded arrests for exhibitionist nudity as well as for brawling.

✚ L21 ✉ East coast, 15km (9 miles) south of Rhodes Town 🍴 Kastri (€€; ➤ 128) 🚌 East side bus, Rhodes–Faliraki–Kalithies, daily (Rimini Square)

HARAKI

The small, custom-built resort of Haraki is pleasantly contained within the gentle crescent of a little bay. There is a shingle and sand beach whose only shortcoming is that it's in full view of a flanking promenade, lined with villas, cafes and tavernas. Haraki stands at the north end of the Bay of Masari and below the ruins of the ancient castle of Feraklos high on its rocky hill. The original Byzantine castle was the first of Rhodes' fortresses to fall to the Knights of St John in 1306, and it became one of the main strongholds on the island until the final Turkish conquest.

You can reach the castle from the north end of Haraki beach by following a concrete road to a water tank, from where rough ground leads up left to a vestigial path to an entrance to the castle's broad inner precincts, now overgrown. Alternatively, a rough track leads from just behind the resort to where a path, then a stone staircase, lead to the entrance. The track continues from this point

past several unfinished and abandoned villas to reach the fine sandy beach of Agia Agathi, popular, but undeveloped. (A signposted track from the coast road to Agia Agathi is best avoided, as it is a long detour and punishing to cars.)

➕ J17 ✉ East coast, 40km (25 miles) south of Rhodes Town

🍴 Da Vinci (€–€€; ➤ 128)

🚌 East side bus, Rhodes–Haraki, daily (Rimini Square)

IALYSSOS

Best places to see, ➤ 42–43.

IXIA

The first tourist beach south of Rhodes Town on the west coast, Ixia has been long established as a resort, though its identity is all but overpowered by the dense surroundings of huge luxury hotels. Every kind of watersport is available on the long, narrow sand and shingle beach. You may feel trapped between the busy coast road and the offshore flight path to Rhodes airport, but if close-quarters sociability and convenience appeals, Ixia has enough to spare.

➕ L23 ✉ West coast, 5km (3 miles) southwest of Rhodes Town

🍴 Le Gourmet (€€; ➤ 128–129) 🚌 West side bus, Rhodes–Paradissi, daily (Averof Street)

KAMIROS

Best places to see, ➤ 46–47.

KOLIMBIA

The resort of Kolimbia is famed for its long approach avenue, lined by towering eucalyptus trees. The Italians built model farms throughout the coastal plain here during the early 20th century; and the planting of the trees was part of a drainage scheme. At the avenue's seaward end it branches; the left branch leads quickly to the small North Beach that is the southern termination of the sweeping Afandou beach. The right-hand branch takes you to a rather barren area of partially excavated sand. There is a small beach here and a harbour sheltering fishing boats. A short distance farther on from here is the larger and more appealing South Beach.

✚ K19 ✉ East coast, 21km (13 miles) south of Rhodes Town ⑪ To Limanaki (€; ➤ 129) 🚌 East side bus, Rhodes–Kolimbia, daily (Rimini Square)

KREMASTI

Kremasti is one of Rhodes' larger villages, where you can capture the mood of everyday Rhodian life in cafes and tavernas. The main focus of the village is the handsome Church of the Panagia, Our Lady of Kremasti, a large building within a complex of mature trees and formal lawns and with a flanking arcade surfaced with superb *hokhláki* (pebble mosaic) flooring. The interior walls are covered in modern icons; there is a splendid golden iconostasis, or altar screen, and extravagant chandeliers. Adjacent to the church is a bone-white classical building that houses a library. This building and the church were funded by donations from expatriate local people, mainly living in America.

✚ K23 ✉ West coast, 13km (8 miles) southwest of Rhodes Town
🍴 Dimosthenas, Leoforos Eleftherias 27 (€) 🚌 West side bus, Rhodes–Kremasti, daily (Averof Street) ❓ Please dress soberly in the church; no photography inside

KRITINIA KASTELLOS

The ruins of the medieval *kastello* of Kritinia stand on top of a 131m (430ft) hill overlooking olive groves and pine woods

above the sea. This was one of the key strategic fortresses of the Knights of St John and the walls once boasted the coats of arms of several Grand Masters. Today the castle is a lonely ruin that

rises through several levels to a final vantage point offering outstanding views. About 3km (2 miles) southeast of the castle is the quiet little village of Kritinia. On the main road above the village is the Kritinia Folklore Museum, which contains an interesting collection of rural artefacts, crafts and traditional dress.

✚ C10 ✉ West coast, 34km (21 miles) southwest of Rhodes Town 🎟 Castle open access, museum variable 🍴 Cafe/taverna at Kritinia (€), snack bar at museum (€) 🚌 West side bus, Rhodes–Kritinia, daily (Averof Street)

LADIKO

Known locally as Anthony Quinn Bay, this area of coastline to the south of Faliraki incorporates two small rock coves with tiny beaches. They are well known and popular but there is minimal development, thus adding to the appeal of crystal clear water and headlands dense with wild shrubs and flowers. The small bay to the south (the first one reached along the approach from the main road) has a little sandy beach. The Anthony Quinn connection relates to the filming of parts of *The Guns of Navarone* that took place in the northerly bay, where there is a rocky foreshore and picturesque cliffs. A pleasant cliff path runs north from here for about 1km (0.6 miles) and leads to the scrubby headland of Cape Ladiko, which overlooks Faliraki's southern beach.

➕ L21 ✉ East coast, 17km (10.5 miles) south of Rhodes Town 🍴 Tavernas/ cafes at both beaches (€) 🚌 East side bus, Rhodes–Afandou (Rimini Square). 1.4km (0.8-mile) walk from coast road junction

PETALOUDES

Best places to see, ➤ 52–53.

PROFITIS ILIAS

Best places to see, ➤ 54–55.

STEGNA

The medium-sized beach at Stegna lies on the coast below the village of Archangelos. It is reached down a road that winds through a raw landscape of limestone pinnacles and cliffs. High rocky hills frame Stegna to north and south, giving some landscape character to the beach. The beach is a sun trap, but its narrowness means that it can become crowded and development is increasing.

➕ K18 ✉ East coast, 36km (22 miles) south of Rhodes Town 🍴 Kozas Taverna (€€–€€€; ➤ 59) 🚌 East side bus, Rhodes–Archangelos, daily (Rimini Square)

a walk

through the pines of Profitis Ilias

This delightful walk follows the landscaped tracks and stone staircases on the wooded summit of Profitis Ilias mountain (➤ 54–55).

From the junction below the kafenío (cafe), follow the rough road to the right, signed Childrens' Camp and Athletic Centre. After about 300m (330yds), look for rocky steps rising through the trees on the right. Leave the road and follow the steps uphill.

The stone staircases of Profitis Ilias were constructed in the 1920s by the Italians as part of a landscaping scheme.

Where the path fades near a bend in the road, bear round sharply right and uphill. In a few metres, pick up the stepped path once more. Follow a mix of broken steps and a stone-lined path through uphill zigzags to reach a good viewpoint.

This is an ideal spot for a picnic. There are sweeping views over the trees to the roofs of Profitis Ilias settlement, and to Salakos.

Follow the path gently downhill to reach a sharp right turn.

Up to the left is the summit of Profitis Ilias, with radio masts; no access to the public.

At a junction (fallen tree) bear sharply left, then right. Keep left and downhill at next faint junction. Descend through zigzags to reach a derelict church. Pass to the

*right of the church then go left and then down steps.
Follow a track for a few metres towards a ruined
villa ahead.*

The villa and church were built for Mussolini during the
Italian occupation of Rhodes.

*Just before the house, go left down rough steps to
the road and turn right to return to your start.*

Distance 3km (2 miles)
Time 1.5 hours
Start/end point Profitis Ilias *kafenío* ✚ F10
Lunch Profitis Ilias *kafenío* (€)

SYMI

The small but mountainous island of Symi lies between the lobster-like claws of Turkish peninsulas. It is a beautiful island, emphatically Greek in nature. The approach by boat to Symi Town reveals a stunning amphitheatre of 19th-century neoclassical houses – an unexpected and breathtaking sight. Evidence of Symi's remarkable past is seen in the numerous ruined and empty buildings that pepper the older parts of the town. Until the early 20th century the island had a population of over 20,000, and was wealthier even than Rhodes because of its lucrative sponge-diving, shipbuilding and sea trade. Then the island's economy was blighted by a combination of the Italian occupation of the Dodecanese, the war between Greece and Turkey, and a rapid decline in the sponge trade. Emigration on a huge scale followed.

Today, Symi is flourishing again, as a result of tourism – it is a very popular day trip from Rhodes. The island's steep-sidedness and a lack of water have ensured that over-development has not happened. Symi Town and the island's outlying districts retain the charm of an older Greece.

Gialos and Chorio (Symi Town)

Symi Town is made up of its lower harbour area, known as Gialos, and the upper, older town known as Chorio. The harbour is broad and long, framed by rising land to either side and overlooked by tiers of pastel-coloured houses with elegant pediments. Ferries and excursion boats mostly dock at the west quay which is lined with cafes, tavernas, shops and workshops. The harbourside road leads on from here to the settlement of Harani, where small boatyards maintain the tradition of Symi boatbuilding.

The older district of Chorio rises dramatically from the east side of the harbour to where a line of old windmills punctuates the skyline and the ruined castle of the Knights of St John, occupied by the Church of Megali Panagia, crowns the highest point. The best way to approach Chorio is to climb the magnificent stone staircase, the Kali Strata, where the atmospheric shells of abandoned 19th-century mansions line the lower stairs. From higher up the Kali Strata you enter a fascinating world where tempting alleyways lead off to either side into a maze of occupied and unoccupied houses linked by stairways and narrow passages (➤ 122–123).

✚ M24 (off map) ✉ 24km (15 miles) north of Rhodes Island 🍴 Fish Restaurant Manos (€€; ➤ 129), Georgio's (€; ➤ 129) 🚌 Hourly bus to Chorio and Pedio from east side of harbour 🚢 Day excursion boats from Rhodes Town, water-taxis to various beaches, May–Oct ❓ Symi Festival Jun–Sep. Music, drama, poetry, folk culture

ℹ️ No tourist office, but English-language newspaper *The Symi Visitor* is an excellent source of information

Moni Taxiarchas Michael Panormitis

The monastery of Panormitis lies at the far southern tip of Symi and is an extremely popular destination for excursion boats. It can be reached by road from Symi Town, but this involves a hard six-hour walk or by taxi. The most convenient – and dramatic – approach is from the sea into the horseshoe-shaped bay that lies in front of Panormitis below pine-covered hills. The 18th-century monastery is a huge building, almost Venetian in style. Its tall, baroque bell tower dominates the long white facade of the main building. The inner courtyard contains the freestanding church, which has a superb carved wooden altar screen and numerous gold and silver lamps. The centrepiece is a silver-leafed icon of the Archangel Michael (patron saint of Symi and protector of sailors) said to work miracles. Devout pilgrims have left votive offerings in hope of salvation. Here you can visit a small Byzantine Museum and there is also a museum of folklore.

✚ M24 (off map) ✉ 14km (9 miles) from Symi Town ⅋ Cafe and taverna (€€) ✋ Museums inexpensive ⛴ Excursion boats from Rhodes and water-taxis from Gialos

Pedio

The small village of Pedio lies on the south side of the high promontory that flanks Symi Town. It still retains its engaging character as a fishing village from where small boats work the inshore waters. There is a narrow shingly beach on the waterfront, but it takes half an hour to walk along the path across the rocky hillside from the south end of the village to the pleasant sandy beach of Agios Nikolaos. A 20-minute walk along a path from the north end of the village leads to the shingle beach of Agios Marina. Both beaches become very busy in summer, as crowded water-taxis arrive from Symi Town.

✚ M24 (off map) ✉ 3km (2 miles) from Symi Town ⅋ Julies Bar, Pedio beach (€) 🚌 Hourly bus from Gialos ⛴ Water-taxis from Gialos

a walk along the stone steps of Chorio

This walk links the two great stone staircases of Chorio and visits Symi's museum and several churches.

From Skala Square climb the broad steps of the Kali Strata. Follow prominent signs (blue arrows) to the museum, through a series of alleyways.

The museum contains an excellent collection of Byzantine and medieval artefacts. Nearby is the restored 18th-century Chatziagapitos Mansion.

Walk straight ahead from the museum doorway past a telegraph pole. Go beneath an arch, then climb steps by a sign for "Castle". Pass a house with blue-painted steps, then follow a narrow alley. At a junction keep right, go down two steps to an open square in front of the handsome Church of Agios Athanosios.

Like all of Symi's churches, St Athanosios is brightly painted and immaculate.

Go down curved steps on the far side of the square, then turn left.

Keep straight ahead at the telegraph pole, then at a T-junction go left. At the next junction go right to reach another immaculate church. Go up the steps to the left of the church, then turn right, then left. Keep ahead to where a sharp turn right leads up some steps. Go up left to reach the castle (Kastro).

The site of the old castle is dominated by the Church of Megali Panagia, a replacement of a previous church destroyed during World War II. One of the church bells is the nose-cone of a bomb.

Retrace your steps from the church, then go down left to reach another church with a tall bell tower. Turn right down more steps, then go left. Follow a road round the hillside to reach another church, from where steps lead down to the top of the Katarraktis, Chorio's second great stone stairway that leads down to Gialos.

Distance 2.5km (1.5 miles)
Time 3 hours, allowing for visits to museum and churches
Start point Skala Square, Gialos
End point Gialos
Lunch Cafes on approach to museum (€)

THERMES KALITHEAS

Reopened in the summer of 2007 following renovation, the spa complex at Kalitheas has finally regained its eccentric appeal. Kalitheas' healing springs were famous as early as the classical period, and the Italians spared no effort in turning the spa into a 1930s mock Ottoman showpiece – a palm-fringed, seaside oasis complete with colonnaded gardens, curving staircases, domed pavilions and pebble mosaic paving. A central cupola, supported by pillars, stands over a circular spa pool. There is a small shingle and sand beach and several rocky coves.

➕ M22 ✉ East coast, 9km (6 miles) south of Rhodes Town ☎ 24410 65691; www.kalitheasprings.gr ⏰ Open daily 8am–7pm 🍴 Seasonal cafe and taverna (€–€€) 👋 Inexpensive 🚌 East side bus, Rhodes–Faliraki (Rimini Square) 🚤 Excursion boats from Mandraki Harbour

TRIANDA

Trianda is a busy and lively village with a local identity. There is a shingle beach about 500m (545yds) from the main road, which is popular in the summer with windsurfers as well as sun lovers, this being the breezier side of the island. Ancient Trianda was essentially the Bronze Age precursor to classical Ialyssos and throughout the broad agricultural plain that spreads inland behind the village, numerous prehistoric artefacts have been found. Trianda's Church of the Dormition of the Virgin has a splendid baroque bell tower.

✚ K23 ✉ West coast, 8km (5 miles) southwest of Rhodes Town
🍴 Ta Kioupia, Ialyssos (€€€; ➤ 128) 🚌 West side bus, Rhodes–Paradissi (Averof Street) ❓ Aug festival

TSAMBIKA

The Tsambika area has two attractions: a surprisingly undeveloped but popular beach, and the monastery of Panagia Tsambika, known also as Kyra, perched on top of a huge cone-shaped hill that towers to a height of 287m (941ft) above the beach. The monastery is reached by a concrete road that twists steeply up from the highway, just before the beach access road. You park just beyond the Panoramic Restaurant and finish the journey on foot up winding stone stairs through pine trees. There are 307 steps, marked at 100-step intervals. The "monastery" is no more than a tiny chapel and courtyard, but the views are spectacular, and the chapel contains a greatly revered icon of the Annunciation that legend says arrived miraculously and inexplicably from Cyprus.

✚ K19 ✉ East coast, 30km (19 miles) south of Rhodes Town 🍴 Seasonal *kantinás* (food and drink stall) and taverna at beach (€). Panoramic Restaurant below monastery (€–€€) 🚌 East side bus, Rhodes–Archangelos (Rimini Square) ❓ Dress soberly when visiting monastery, no photography inside. 8 Sep, Festival during which childless women climb up to the monastery to pray for a baby. If they are successful, the child is named Tsambikos or Tsambika

HOTELS

AFANDOU
Lippia Hotel Golf Resort (€€€)

All-inclusive 4-star hotel and resort complex with rooms and suites, most overlooking the sea and/or the golf course, with plenty of family-friendly activities, restaurant and shops.

✉ Afandou ☎ 22410 52007; www.rhotel.gr ⊘ Closed Nov–Apr

ARCHANGELOS (STEGNA)
Panorama Stegna (€)

Panorama offers rooms and studios, each with a balcony, plus a cafe (with WiFi and satellite television) serving light meals. It lies in Stegna, 3km (2 miles) from Archangelos.

✉ Stegna ☎ 22440 22516; www.stegna.gr ⊘ Closed Nov–Apr

FALIRAKI
Esperides Beach Hotel (€€€)

A large, modern beachfront hotel with a swimming pool. Well equipped for family holidays and offering every facility, including a cocktail bar, disco, mini-market, coffee bar, poolside taverna, tennis courts, mini-golf and volleyball. For youngsters there are numerous attractions ranging from bumper cars to a Venturer simulator.

✉ Faliraki ☎ 22410 85267; email: info@esperia-hotels.gr ⊘ Closed Nov–Mar

IXIA
Atlantic Princess Hotel (€€)

A good choice for a fun family holiday, this 4-star hotel has a big lagoon-shaped outdoor pool, a gym and a wellness centre offering sauna and massage. There are organized activities for both adults and children and it's only a short walk from the beach.

✉ Ixia ☎ 22410 96100; www.atlanticahotels.com ⊘ Closed Dec–Mar

KOLIMBIA
Kolimbia Star (€€)

This 3-star hotel has clean modern rooms, a pool rimmed with sun beds and a separate pool and playground for children. There are

tennis and volleyball courts all set within landscaped gardens.
It lies just a three-minute walk from the beach.

✉ Kolimbia ☎ 22410 56600; www.kolymbiastar.gr ⊘ Closed Nov–Mar

LADIKO
Hotel Cathrin (€€–€€€)

Very smart and beautifully located 4-star hotel, entirely on its
own with sea views. Caters well for families with a swimming
pool, children's pool and playroom and a selection activities.

✉ Ladiko ☎ 22410 85080; www.cathrinhotel.gr ⊘ Closed Nov–Mar

SYMI
Hotel Fiona (€)

Pleasant small hotel with a pool and breakfast terrace. Unrivalled
position with great harbour views from front-facing rooms. Free
WiFi offered to guests.

✉ Top of Kali Strata, Chorio ☎ 22460 72088; www.fionahotel.com

The Little Owl (€€)

Rent your own little house in Symi, by the day, close to the harbour
but elevated to give sea views and a feel of really living in Greece,
with your own kitchen.

✉ Gialos, behind Alpha Bank ☎ 22460 71785;
www.symivisitor.com/littleowl.htm

Villa Karnayo (€€)

In the area near the old boatyards but a steep climb up is this 2- to
3-person villa with kitchen. The balcony offers superb views of the
harbour and the town centre is only a 10-minute walk away.

✉ Harani, Symi Town ☎ 22460 71785; www.symivisitor.com/karnayo.htm

TRIANDA
Electra Palace Hotel (€€€€)

Modern superior 5-star resort hotel with 308 rooms and good
amenities; popular with families.

✉ Trianda Beach ☎ 22410 92521; www.electrahotels.gr ⊘ Closed
Nov–Mar

RESTAURANTS

ARCHANGELOS
Savas (€€)
A friendly atmosphere in this pleasant taverna right on the busy main street. Menu includes top of the range lobster, stuffed squid and reliable meat dishes. Quite pricey, but excellent. Rhodian wines available as well as decent and inexpensive house wine.
✉ Archangelos ☎ 22440 23125 🕓 Lunch, dinner

FALIRAKI
Kastri (€€)
Fresh oven-cooked pizzas are a popular choice in this otherwise very Greek taverna which is as popular with locals (they cater for weddings and parties) as it is with visitors.
✉ Near Calypso Hotel, Faliraki ☎ 22410 85381; www.kastri-restaurant.com
🕓 Daily lunch and dinner

HARAKI
Da Vinci (€–€€)
One block back from the seafront, this Italian restaurant serves generous portions at very reasonable prices. Look for the house specials, including meat and seafood dishes in rich creamy sauces.
✉ Haraki ☎ 22440 51460 🕓 Varies according to season

IALYSSOS
Ta Kioupia (€€€)
In the candlelit courtyard garden of a stone mansion, on a hill affording great views of Ialyssos Bay, is Ta Kioupia, among the top restaurants in Greece. Creative dishes are prepared from fresh local produce. Reservations recommended.
✉ Argonayton 12, Ialyssos ☎ 22410 93448; www.takioupia.com 🕓 Varies according to season

IXIA
Le Gourmet (€€)
This family-run eatery, off the main coastal strip in a side street next to the Miramare Wonderland Resort, serves traditional and

tasty Greek specialities. It's popular with locals and tourists alike who come for the authentic flavours of Greece.

✉ Kandalou ☎ 22410 90829 ⏰ Varies according to season

KAMIROS
Taverna Old Kamiros (€)

Standard Greek cooking is on the menu at this roadside taverna, but choose one of the tasty fish dishes done in oil or grilled for a good value meal. There's also a wide selection of salads.

✉ Kamiros ☎ 22410 40012; www.oldkamiros.com ⏰ Lunch, dinner

KAMIROS SKALA
Althaimeni (€€)

This fish restaurant comes well recommended by locals. A sunny outdoor terrace overlooks the fishing harbour. A big menu includes such expensive treats as red mullet and lobster. For starters try fried aubergines. Check out the good salads and dips.

✉ Kamiros Skala ☎ 22460 31303 ⏰ Lunch, dinner

KOLIMBIA
To Limanaki (€)

Long-established fish taverna offering good selection of fresh fish dishes. In a good position overlooking beach.

✉ Kolimbia ☎ 22410 56240 ⏰ All day

SYMI
Fish Restaurant Manos (€€)

Excellent fish restaurant offering a big menu that includes oysters, clams, king prawns, lobster, and much more. Try Symi shrimps for starters. Reservations advised.

✉ Harbourside, Gialos ☎ 22460 72429 ⏰ Lunch, dinner

Georgio's (€)

High up the Kali Strata, Georgio's is a taverna with character – and characters in plenty. The food's quite good too. The fish soup makes an excellent starter, but then you may get it as a finisher.

✉ Kali Strata, Chorio ☎ 22460 71984 ⏰ Most days

Mylopetra (€€€)

Based in an old mill, this gourmet restaurant serves creative Mediterranean cuisine prepared from fresh local ingredients. Expect exquisite lamb and seafood dishes, as well as home-made bread and pasta.

✉ Gialos harbour ☎ 22410 72333; www.mylopetra.com

🕒 May–Oct, dinner only

SHOPPING

FOOD AND DRINK

Anastasia Triantafillou Vineyard and Wine Cellar

This independent (and very friendly) winery has superb vintages from organically produced local Athiri grapes and Cabernet Sauvignon. Every bottle is good, but splash out on Kalos Aygos, the vineyard's finest. They also produce superb moscatel.

✉ Petaloudes (on approach road from main west coast road. Signed on right-hand side of road along track) ☎ 22410 82041 🕒 Daily 10–8

GIFTS

En Plo

A small store stocking handmade wooden objects, including miniature boats.

✉ Gialos, Symi ☎ 22460 70071

Loukidis Jewellery

Symi's only jewellery designer handcrafts pieces from gold and precious stones. Loukidis lies at the beginning of Kali Strata, near the harbourfront.

✉ Gialos, Symi ☎ 22460 72249

ENTERTAINMENT

Bed Club

Sometimes very good, sometimes average, but Bed's famous foam parties will be right over your head. Expect guest DJs from the UK and a dance floor hosting up to 2,000 revellers. Dress down.

✉ Faliraki 🕒 24 hours

Chalki

□ Lindos

Southern Rhodes

Beyond Rhodes Town lies a different world which, in the far south especially, offers a fascinating contrast to the urban and resort areas.

On the west coast there is a thinning out of development once past the airport, and soon this more remote coastline is dominated by the island's forested mountain chain. The east coast is developed as far as Lindos, but beyond there you again encounter an island that seems entirely separate from the busy, popular Rhodes of the brochures. Inland there is yet another world of olive groves and scrub-covered hills that shelter charming villages. You can explore island Rhodes by bus, or more independently by car, and there are good opportunities to walk along remote beaches and in the mountains.

ASKLIPIO

Best places to see, ➤ 40–41.

CHALKI

The small island of Chalki is an elusive place, well out of the mainstream network of inter-island ferries. The island makes for a pleasant extended stay although not a beach-orientated one; the handful of sand beaches and pebbled coves can become very crowded in summer due to package holiday-makers who rent villas here. Once dependent on sponge fishing, the island suffered heavy depopulation due to a dramatic decline in the industry during the early 1900s. Today many of the abandoned houses of the port settlement of Niborio have been converted into holiday villas. There are no buses or vehicle rental on the island.

✚ B12 (inset) ✉ 15km (9 miles) west of Rhodes Island 🍴 Mavri Thalassa, Chalki harbourfront (€€) ⛴ Ferries from Kamiros Skala and from Mandraki but usually involve at least an overnight stay

GENNADI

The village of Gennadi is the last sizeable settlement before the remoter reaches of the far south. Gennadi is an unassuming village with a great deal of charm, and its villagers enhance this with their engaging friendliness. Located on the rising ground above the coast road, the village is a pleasing jumble of white-painted houses traversed by long narrow streets. In the northwest area is the Church of Agios Ioannis, located within a complex of old buildings that surrounds a *hokhláki* (pebble mosaic floored) courtyard with a central cypress tree. On the way to the church is a beautifully refurbished olive-pressing barn, complete with equipment (flexible opening times). Gennadi's beach is a very long stretch of sand and gravel, which shelves away a short distance offshore.

✚ E4 ✉ Southeast coast, 77km (48 miles) south of Rhodes Town ❚❚ Mama's Kitchen (€–€€; ➤ 151) 🚌 East side bus, Rhodes–Kattavia (Rimini Square)

GLYSTRA

The sandy crescent of Glystra beach is a surprising treat amid a coastline of barren rock, alongside the undeveloped stretch of road south of Lardos. It is not empty, however, as it is very accessible and irresistible to anyone driving by. The sand is clean and silky and the beach is backed by tree-studded dunes. South of Glystra, the

rocky shoreline can be reached from the roadside in several places, but be careful of loose rock and shale when you are descending.

✚ G15 ✉ East coast, 69km (43 miles) south of Rhodes Town ❚❚ Seasonal snack bar (€) 🚌 East side bus, Rhodes–Asklipio, also Rhodes–Kattavia (Rimini Square)

KASTROU MONOLITHOS

Best places to see, ➤ 48–49.

KATTAVIA

When you reach Kattavia, you feel as if you have truly escaped from the rest of Rhodes. This is no historical backwater, though, as there has been a settlement here from ancient times (remains from the Mycenaean period have been found). The Italians left their inevitable mark in the shape of model farms amid the flat fields of the area. Just before reaching the village you pass the derelict Italian-era farm of Agios Pavlos with its church tower

of San Paolo. The central crossroads in Kattavia is a great local meeting place and has several cafes and tavernas. In the Byzantine church of the Dormition of the Virgin there are fine 17th-century frescoes. The Church of St Paraskevi has a flamboyant and vividly coloured bell-tower.

🔳 C3 ✉ Southwest coast, 96km (60 miles) south of Rhodes Town 🍴 Restaurant Penelope (€–€€) 🚌 East side bus, Rhodes–Kattavia (Rimini Square)

KIOTARI

The beach resort of Kiotari was once the coastal settlement of Asklipio before the community moved inland during the Byzantine period to escape repeated pirate raids. Today Kiotari is given over entirely to tourism. The northern section of the beach has the most character. A tiny cane-built hut still crowns the small rock promontory of Hilioravdi, the Rock of One Thousand Stakes – a reference to a medieval incident during which local people sowed the beach with sharpened stakes as a defence against pirate landings. The hut was built by a local schoolteacher and his pupils over 50 years ago.

🔳 F5 ✉ East coast, 62km (38 miles) south of Rhodes Town 🍴 Stefano (€€; ➤ 151) 🚌 East side bus, Rhodes–Kiotári, daily (Rimini Square)

LAHANIA

Hidden amid deep green countryside, the peaceful village of Lahania is another of those remote settlements whose origins may date as far back as the Bronze Age. Many of Lahania's delightful 19th-century houses have been restored. Wander down through the village from the upper approach road to reach the tiny square. Its solitary taverna and detached church tower are overshadowed by an enormous plane tree. Two fountains add a refreshing murmur to the square; one has a surviving Ottoman inscription. Just up from the square, following the left-hand exit, stands an old restored mill.

🕂 D3 ✉ East coast, 88km (55 miles) south of Rhodes Town 🍴 Taverna Platanos, main square (€) 🚌 East side bus, Rhodes–Kattavia (Rimini Square)

LARDOS

The inland village of Lardos has a busy commercial life, but it still caters for holidaymakers, and there are lots of tavernas, cafes and music bars clustered round its broad central junction. At the centre of this junction is an art deco fountain, a legacy of the Italian era. The village has an excellent fish market and a number of useful shops. The Church of Agios Taxiarchas is tucked away in the older part of the village and is an impressive building with a big bell tower and tall cypress trees crowding its entrance courtyard. Every building in the old village seems to have a lemon tree in its garden, and there are some vividly painted doors and frames. Lardos beach is about 2km (1.2 miles) south and is fairly mundane, but undeveloped.

H15 ⊠ East coast, 55km (34 miles) south of Rhodes Town 🍽 Mr Danton, Lindian Village Hotel (€€€) 🚌 East side bus, Rhodes–Lardos (Rimini Square) ❓ Please dress soberly in the church; no photography inside

LINDOS

Lindos is an impossibly picturesque village; a labyrinth of white-painted Dodecanesian-style houses climbing the slopes to the dramatic Acropolis and Knights' castle. The village is, of course, a hugely popular visitor attraction, and from Easter onwards it is crowded by day and fairly lively by night. The Acropolis (▶ 36–37) is the main attraction, but Lindos has much more to offer than this splendid monument. Its narrow streets are empty of traffic and locals carry everything in motorbike trailers with which they negotiate some alarming challenges amid the steeper streets. In some ways Lindos is robbed of its inherent character by the sheer pressure of visitors and by the "guided tour" atmosphere that dominates proceedings – in several languages. Yet the village is still captivating, especially if you allow time to wander and seek out less well-known ancient ruins, the tiny churches, and the quieter corners.

Ancient Lindos was the most prestigious of the three great city-states of Rhodes, the others being Kamiros (► 46–47) and Ialyssos (► 42–43). When the three cities combined to found the unified city of Rhodes, Lindos continued to prosper; its sanctuary of Lindian Athena remained a place of pilgrimage until Roman times. The Knights of St John kept a strong presence here, and during the Turkish era, Lindos was a prosperous seagoing community. Modern Lindos still reflects this history of commerce and culture.

➕ J15 ✉ East coast, 56km (35 miles) south of Rhodes Town 🍴 Agostino's (€–€€; ➤ 152) or Mythos (€€; ➤ 152) 🚌 East side bus, Rhodes–Lindos (Rimini Square) 🛈 Municipal Tourist Office, Plateia Eleftherias, tel: 22440 31900; May–Sep 8am–9pm

Akropoli

Best places to see, ➤ 36–37.

Ancient Sites

The prime site of the Acropolis apart, there are a number of other ancient sites scattered throughout the Lindos area. Within the village itself is the well-preserved 4th-century BC amphitheatre. It is located on the southwestern side of the Acropolis just below the Stavri Square car park. Nearby are the remains of a large building, thought to have been a temple of the 3rd or 2nd century BC. Later Christian churches were built over the site. Directly opposite the Acropolis, on the side of Krana Hill and above the highest houses of the village, is the ruin of a monumental necropolis, the tomb of a wealthy Hellenistic family. On Cape Agios Emilianos, across the main bay from the Acropolis, is the so-called Tomb of Kleoboulos, a large circular mausoleum composed of stone slabs. It can be reached by a path from the main beach. There is no convincing evidence that this is actually the tomb of Kleoboulos, a famous ruler of Lindos.

Beaches

On the north side of the village is a substantial bay in the shelter of the Acropolis hill. Directly below the Acropolis lies a small harbour where fishing boats moor. Farther round the bay is Lindos's very busy main beach. There are several tavernas and bars, beach furniture can be hired and watersports are available. There is another beach farther round the bay, and bathing places beyond the headland of Cape Agios Emilianos. To the south of the Acropolis lies the remarkable natural harbour of St Paul, where the evangelist is said to have landed on his mission to spread Christianity.

Panagia (Church of the Assumption of our Lady)

Panagia is the main church of Lindos and stands at the heart of the village. It dates from medieval times but has been lovingly cared for and refurbished over the years. The characteristic exterior is rather engulfed by its close-knit surroundings but the interior is overwhelming, a superb example of Orthodox decoration. Late 19th-century frescoes, restored in the 1920s, cover the walls and depict vivid biblical scenes. There are numerous fine icons, and the wooden altar screen and Bishop's throne are beautifully carved. The pebble mosaic floor is outstanding. There is a strict requirement for visitors to dress soberly, and photography is not allowed.

Spitia ton Kapetanion (Houses of the Captains)

An earthquake of 1610 devastated Lindos but the settlement was rebuilt in traditional style, and today's houses, a mix of simple vernacular buildings and handsome Gothic mansions, enhanced with subtle Byzantine and Moorish features, stand behind their high walls and inner courtyards where there is much use made of the exquisite pebble flooring called *hokhláki*. The Lindian doorways, called *pyliónes*, often have fine carving on their doorcases and pediments. Wealth from seagoing enriched Lindos, and many of the finer houses were built by sea captains. Several of these restored captains' houses are open for public viewing, although they are often tied in with restaurants or gift shops. You can get details from the tourist office.

141

MONI THARI

Deep inland at the centre of Rhodes lies the monastery of the Archangel Michael at Thari. It is reached from the pleasant village of Laerma. You follow the road through Laerma and after about 50m (55yds) keep left at an unsignposted junction. Continue along an unsurfaced but reasonable track for about 4km (2.5 miles) through pleasantly wooded countryside, following signs to the monastery. Moni Thari is said to be the oldest religious foundation on the island and ruins within the grounds date from the 9th century. Today's monastery is run on thoroughly modern lines, however, and it even has its own television channel and a

triple belfry with seven electronically operated bells. Inside
the handsome Byzantine church, traditional Orthodoxy is
vividly expressed through the splendid frescoes and
carved wooden altar piece.

➕ E7 ✉ East coast, 84km (52 miles) southwest of Rhodes Town
🍴 Small snack bar at entrance (€) 🚌 East side bus, Rhodes–
Laerma (Rimini Square) ❓ Please dress soberly if visiting the
monastery – smocks are provided for anyone in shorts or brief tops.
No photography inside

PEFKOS

In many ways the beach resort of Pefkos has become a
dormitory suburb of Lindos. The resort developed where
only olive groves and a few fishermen's houses once
stood. There are now numerous villas and small hotels
with attendant tavernas, bars and shops. Most are low key
and Pefkos is fairly quiet, relative to Rhodes' more frenetic
resorts. There is a string of small, pleasant, sandy beaches
along the sheltered bay on which Pefkos stands.

➕ J15 ✉ East coast, 60km (37 miles) south of Rhodes Town
🍴 Enigma (€–€€; ➤ 153). Cafes and tavernas on approach road
to beach (€) 🚌 East side bus, Rhodes–Pefkos (Rimini Square)

PLIMIRI

You need to make an effort to reach this fine beach in the far south of Rhodes, but the chance of having some space to yourself is the reward. The absence of development is another bonus and the only activity is at the concrete quay where fishing boats moor overnight. Plimiri's beach runs in a long elegant curve and fringes a shallow bay between the fishing quay and the narrow Cape Germata in the south. At the north end of the beach is the rather stark white building of the Monastery of Zoodohos Pigi (Source of Life), an

intriguing structure that dates from the 1840s and is built over the ruins of an early Christian church. Incorporated into the exterior of the monastery are classical columns with Corinthian capitals.

✚ D2 ✉ East coast, 90km (56 miles) south of Rhodes Town 🍴 Seasonal taverna (€)

On Rhodes you are never too far from beach, bar or boutique, but at every step you move amid the haunting relics and legacies of the island's vivid past. Few Mediterranean islands can match its mix of indulgent holiday-making and rewarding culture: a world of good food and drink, the promise of escape to nearby islands such as Symi and Chalki, the cool solitude of the mountains, the luxury of hidden coves, the blue Aegean, and the unstinting hospitality of some of the friendliest and most generous people in the world.

PRASONISI

The lonely cape of Akra Praso lies at the most southerly point of Rhodes on the hilly promontory of Prasonisi. The cape is connected to the mainland by a broad sand bar that is awash during the winter months when there is a rise in sea level and when wind-driven swells roll across the bar. In summer the sand bar is exposed and creates a choice of beach venues to either side; fresh and breezy for windsurfing on the northwest shore, quieter waters for sunbathing on the eastern side. The mainland beach at Prasonisi is enormous: a vast, flat expanse of hard-packed sand, with softer sand

along the water's edge. Development is increasing, but the beach is big enough to cope with it.

✚ B1 ✉ South coast, 105km (65 miles) southwest of Rhodes Town 🍴 Restaurants and cafe-bars at entrance to beach (€)

🚌 East side bus, Rhodes–Prasonisi (Rimini Square), seasonal service

a drive in the far south of Rhodes

The far south and west of Rhodes is pleasingly remote, and this drive follows a rewarding route between the mountains and the sea.

Leave Lindos on the Pefkos road. Bypass Pefkos (▶ 143), or drop off for a swim, and after about 4km (2.5 miles), just before Lardos (▶ 136), turn left up a short link road, signed Gennadi and Kattavia, then turn left onto the main coast road.

From now on, beach resorts thin out and a more remote rural island begins to emerge. Tempting beaches at Glystra (▶ 63, 133) and Plimiri (▶ 63, 144) are easily reached from the main road.

Pass the pleasant villages of Kiotari (▶ 134) and Gennadi (▶ 133), both with good beaches. Continue to Kattavia (▶ 134), beyond which the road swings to the north and the sea comes into view.

For the next 10km (6 miles) there are virtually no buildings. The shore is lined with grey, pebbly beaches backed by low scrub. It can be quite breezy.

At Apolakkia, turn left, signed Monolithos. Continue through pleasant tree-studded countryside to reach Monolithos.

Take some time to explore Monolithos village (▶ 49) for an insight into the rural life of Rhodes away from the tourist attractions.

Turn left at a junction by Cristos Corner taverna and follow the road to Monolithos castle and then downhill to Fourni if you have time. Return to Monolithos, and from the junction by Cristos Corner retrace your route to Apolakkia. From the centre of Apolakkia, take the road, signed Genadi (sic). At a big junction go left, signed Genadi (sic), cross a bridge then continue through low hills to reach a junction with the main coast road at Gennadi. Turn left and return to Lindos via Pefkos.

Distance 130km (80 miles)
Time 6 hours, if beach diversions are made
Start/end point Lindos ✚ J15
Lunch Cristos Corner taverna (€; ➤ 152)

SIANA

The village of Siana stands on the south-facing side of the 823m-high (2,700ft) Mount Akramytis, below forested slopes from which limestone cliffs soar into the sky. Siana is famed for its exquisite honey and its grape distillate, *soumá*. Siana honey has a distinctive flavour, imparted by the herbs and mountain flowers on which the bees feed. Production of *soumá* is prohibited throughout Greece, but Siana benefits from an Italian-era licence that is still extant, allowing the villagers to sell this powerful drink. The impressive single-aisled Church of Agios Pandeliemon lies at the heart of the village just below the main road. There is good walking to be had in the area, but venturing onto the higher reaches of Mount Akramytis requires experience in hill walking and rock scrambling.

✚ C7 ✉ West coast, 50km (31 miles) southwest of Rhodes Town 🍴 Cafes and tavernas in main street (€–€€) 🚌 West side bus, Rhodes–Monolithos (Averof Street)

VLICHA

The attractive crescent beach at Vlicha tends to be monopolized by guests from the large hotels that occupy the land behind the shoreline, but there are plenty of facilities here that can be enjoyed by day visitors. To the north of the headland is a 6km (4-mile) shingle beach that runs from the roadside resort of Kalathos to Charaki, fringing Reni Bay.

✚ J16 ✉ East coast, 52km (32 miles) south of Rhodes Town ⁑ Seasonal *kantinás* (food and drink stalls) and tavernas behind the beach

HOTELS

GENNADI
Effie's Dreams (€)
Tucked away in quiet tree shaded area at the back of the village, just below the Church of Agios Ioannis. Run by a local family, there is a cafe/snack bar attached and Internet facilities.
✉ Gennadi ☎ 22440 43410; www.effiesdreams.com

KIOTARI
Sea Breeze Apartments and Studios (€)
These apartments are in a superb location overlooking the sea and in a quiet position at the north end of Kiotari. They have well-designed and sparkling interiors and are equipped with kitchen, TV, radio, fridge and either a balcony or a veranda.
✉ Kiotari Beach ☎ 22410 69141; www.seabreeze-rhodes.com

LAHANIA
Hotel Lahania (€)
Small, pleasant eight room hotel in a very quiet location on the approach road to the village. The nearest beach is some distance away so your own transport is advisable.
✉ Lahania ☎ 22440 46000/46121

LINDOS
Filoxenia Guesthouse (€€)
There are five double rooms and three suites in this delightful guesthouse right in Lindos Village. Decorated with charming antique furniture, old mirrors and traditional mosaic floors. There is also a courtyard used for breakfast.
✉ Lindos Village ☎ 22440 32080; www.lindos-filoxenia.com

Lindos Bay Hotel (€€–€€€)
Custom-built 4-star hotel with 192 rooms some distance from Lindos itself. Dominates Vlicha Beach, but completely self-contained with a tiny bay below. Superb facilities throughout and with all activities catered for.
✉ Lindos ☎ 22440 32003; www.lindosbay.gr ⊙ Closed Nov–Mar

MONOLITHOS
Hotel Thomas (€)
This straightforward modern complex in the village of Monolithos has nine sizeable rooms that have cooking facilities. It's one of only a few where-to-stay options in this area of Rhodes.

✉ Monolithos ☎ 22460 21291; www.thomashotel.gr

PEFKOS
Pefkos Beach Hotel (€€)
In the heart of Pefkos, near the beach, this big modern complex of self-catering studios and apartments is ideal for families. It has two big pools, two kids' pools, a restaurant, a snack bar and a cocktail bar.

✉ Pefkos ☎ 22440 48008; www.pefkosbeach.gr 🕐 Closed Nov–Apr

VLICHA
Atrium Palace Thalasso Spa Resort and Villas (€€€)
Luxury 5-star hotel in spectacular kitsch design. Utterly exclusive, since no other buildings within sight. Pool complex complete with exotic palms, waterfalls and bridges. Huge adjoining beach.

✉ Kalathos Beach ☎ 22440 31601; www.atrium.gr 🕐 Closed Nov–Mar

RESTAURANTS

GENNADI
Mama's Kitchen (€–€€)
Very pleasant restaurant at heart of village. Great selection of Greek dishes. Try *pitaroudia*, fried chick peas, or *soutzoukakia*, meatballs in delicious sauce. Pizza fanciers are well-catered for too. Good selection of Rhodian wines.

✉ Gennadi ☎ 22440 43547 🕐 Lunch, dinner

KIOTARI
Stefano (€€)
Enjoy your grilled octopus or a tasty seafood platter at this beachside taverna in laid-back Kiotari. The perfect choice for a seafood lunch after a morning of swimming or sunbathing.

✉ Kiotari Beach Road ☎ 22440 47339 🕐 Noon–11pm

LINDOS
Agostino's (€–€€)
Popular with locals and visitors alike, Agostino's is just below the Stavri Square car park with stunning views of the Acropolis. The food is traditional and features tasty dishes such as lamb *kleftikó* (casserole).

✉ Lindos ☎ 22440 31218 🕑 Lunch, dinner

Arhontiko (€€€)
Superb gourmet restaurant in an old sea captain's house, the atmosphere is more than matched by the delicious food with dishes such as steak with dates, sun-dried tomatoes and hazelnuts.

✉ Lindos ☎ 22440 31713; www.arhontikolindos.com 🕑 Daily, dinner only

Broccolino (€–€€)
This relaxed restaurant serves delicious home-made pasta, seasonal salads and oven-baked pizza in a homely courtyard garden with stylish decor and great views. Very popular, so reservations are recommended.

✉ On the road down to Palace Beach ☎ 22440 31668 🕑 Varies according to season

Mythos (€€)
With its several terraces and large rooftop dining area, and excellent views of the lit-up Acropolis at night, the Mythos is understandably busy. The menu includes some Italian dishes as well as Greek staples and there is also a decent wine list. Friendly welcome and excellent service.

✉ Lindos Square ☎ 22440 31300; www.mythoslindos.com 🕑 Daily, dinner only

MONOLITHOS
Cristos Corner (€)
Unmissable on the approach road into Monolithos, this classic rural taverna offers good *mezédhes* and generous charcoal-grilled main dishes. Try yoghurt with the delicious local honey for dessert.

✉ Monolithos ☎ 22460 61310 🕑 Lunch, dinner

PEFKOS
Enigma (€–€€)
This popular double-level bar-restaurant serves meals on an open-air terrace, decorated with plants in big terracotta urns up top, and cocktails in the bar down below.

✉ Pefkos ☎ 22440 48210; www.enigma-pefkos.gr ⏰ Varies according to season

SHOPPING

ARTS AND CRAFTS
Despoina Tharenou
Everything produced in Siana is available at this delightful shop, where the service is charming. Carpets, needlework, ceramics and lace jostle with jars of delicious local honey and the local grape distillate *soumá*.

✉ Siana ☎ 22460 61398

FOOD AND DRINK
Gelo Blu
Mouthwatering Italian ice cream at the heart of Lindos. Everything from pistachio flavour to standard vanilla, as it really should taste.

✉ Lindos ☎ 22440 31761

Lardos Fish Market
If you're self-catering, head for this well-stocked market with its excellent selection of fresh fish and seafood.

✉ Lardos ☎ 22440 44013 ⏰ Mon–Sat 7–2, 5–9

NIGHTLIFE

LINDOS
Amphitheatre Club
One of the island's top nightclubs, with the capacity for up to 2,000 partygoers. It stands just off the main road, on the hill above Lindos, so the noise doesn't spoil the peace and quiet of the town below.

✉ Lindos ☎ 22440 44789; www.amphitheatreclublindos.com

Index

Acknowledgements

The Automobile Association would like to thank the following photographers, companies and picture libraries for their assistance in the preparation of this book.

Abbreviations for the picture credits are as follows – (t) top; (b) bottom; (c) centre; (l) left; (r) right; (AA) AA World Travel Library.

4l Old Town, Rhodes, AA/S Day; **4c** Thermes Kalithea, AA/D Hannigan; **4r** Monastery, Ialyssos, AA/J A Tims; **5l** Monte Smith, AA/S Day; **5r** Mandraki harbour, AA/S Day; **6/7** Old Town, Rhodes, AA/S Day; **8/9** Hippocrates Square, Old Town of Rhodes, AA/S Day; **10t** Roadside monument, AA/J A Tims; **10b** Agaves, AA/S Day; **11tl** Greek Orthodox priest, AA/T L Carlsen; **11tr** Door, Rhodes Town, AA/D Hannigan; **11bl** Turkish Baths, AA/S Day; **11br** Roadside flowers, AA/J A Tims; **12t** Market, AA/J A Tims; **12bl** Greek Salad, AA/J A Tims; **12br** Market, AA/J A Tims; **12/3** Street vendor, AA/J A Tims; **13t** Mezze, AA/J A Tims; **13b** Stifado, AA/J A Tims; **14t** Retsina and calamary, AA/J A Tims; **14c** Swordfish, AA/J A Tims; **14b** Wine bottles at the Emery winery, AA/J A Tims; **14/5** Fish Market, AA/A Mockford & N Bonetti; **15** Emery winery, AA/J A Tims; **16** Lindos Town, AA/J A Tims; **16/7t** Greek coffee, AA/J A Tims; **16/7b** Monolithos, AA/T L Carlsen; **17** Captain's House in Lindos, AA/J A Tims; **18** Café, AA/J A Tims; **19t** Acropolis in Lindos, AA/J A Tims; **19cl** Kameiros, AA/J A Tims; **19cr** Retsina and calamary, AA/J A Tims; **19b** Afantou beach, AA/J A Tims; **20/1** Thermes Kalithea, AA/D Hannigan; **25** Religious procession, AA/P Enticknap; **27** Bus stop sign, AA/T L Carlsen; **28** Roadside monument, AA/J A Tims; **30** Telephone box, AA/J A Tims; **31** Policeman, AA/J A Tims; **34/5** Monastery, Ialyssos, AA/J A Tims; **36t** Acropolis, Lindos, AA/J A Tims; **36b** Acropolis, Lindos, AA/J A Tims; **36/7** Acropolis, Lindos, AA/J A Tims; **37** View from Acropolis, Lindos, AA/J A Tims; **38t** Palace of the Grand Masters, AA/D Hannigan; **38b** Marble inlay at Palace of the Grand Masters, AA/J A Tims; **38/9** Cloisters at Palace of the Grand Masters, AA/J A Tims; **39t** Courtyard of the Palace of the Grand Masters, AA/J A Tims; **39b** Architectural detail at the Palace of the Grand Masters, AA/J A Tims; **40/1t** The church of the Dormition of the Virgin in Asklipeio, AA/D Hannigan; **40/1b** Frescoes in the church of the Dormition of the Virgin in Asklipeio, AA/J A Tims; **41t** Frescoes in the church of the Dormition of the Virgin in Asklipeio, AA/J A Tims; **41b** Castle ruins at Asklipeio, AA/J A Tims; **42t** Interior of Church of Our Lady in Ialyssos, AA/J A Tims; **42b** Fresco in the Church of Our Lady in Ialyssos, AA/J A Tims; **42/3** Bell tower of the Church of Our Lady in Ialyssos, AA/J A Tims; **43t** Column ruins at the Temple of Athena in Ialyssos, AA/J A Tims; **44t** Street of the Knights in Rhodes Town, AA/J A Tims; **44b** Street of the Knights in Rhodes Town, AA/J A Tims; **44/5** Street of the Knights in Rhodes Town, AA/S Day; **45** Crocodile waterspout in Street of the Knights, Rhodes Town, AA/J A Tims; **46** Archaeological remains at Kameiros, AA/J A Tims; **46/7** Archaeological remains at Kameiros, AA/J A Tims; **47** Detail of the Archaeological remains at Kameiros, AA/J A Tims; **48** Stone staircase to St Panteleimon in Monolithos, AA/J A Tims; **48/9t** Fourni beach, Monolithos, AA/J A Tims; **48/9b** Monopetra crag with Monolithos Castle, AA/J A Tims; **50** Medieval Town of Rhodes, towards the Church of Agia Triada, AA/J A Tims; **50/1** Medieval Town of Rhodes, AA/J A Tims; **52l** Petaloudes Valley, AA/J A Tims; **52r** Petaloudes Valley, AA/J A Tims; **52b** Monastery church of Kaliopetra in Petaloudes, AA/D Hannigan; **53** Petaloudes Valley, AA/J A Tims; **54t** Frescoes in Agios Nikolaos Fountoukli church on Profitis Ilias mountain, AA/J A Tims; **54b** Profitis Ilias mountain, AA/J A Tims; **54/5** Steps following a walk through the woods on Profitis Ilias mountain, AA/D Hannigan; **55** Goat on Profitis Ilias mountain, AA/J A Tims; **56/7** Monte Smith, AA/S Day; **58** Taverna in Pefkos, Colinspics/Alamy; **60** Mandraki harbour, AA/J A Tims; **61** Excursion boat, Mandraki harbour, AA/D Hannigan; **62** Glystra beach, AA/J A Tims; **63** Beach in Tsampika, AA/J A Tims; **64/5** Monastery of Panagia Tsampika, AA/J A Tims; **66/7** Kitesurfing, AA/J A Tims; **68/9** The Water Park in Faliraki, The Water Park Faliraki; **69** Go Karting, Faliraki, AA/J A Tims; **70** Italianate buildings, Eleoussa, AA/J A Tims; **70/1** Art Deco fountain in Eleoussa, AA/J A Tims; **71** Church in main square, Eleoussa, AA/J A Tims; **72/3** Mandraki Harbour, AA/S Day; **75** Old Jewish Quarter, AA/J A Tims; **77** Municipal Art Gallery, AA/J A Tims; **78** Rhodes Aquarium, AA/D Hannigan; **78/9** Municipal Baths, AA/J A Tims; **80** Old Jewish Quarter, Rhodes Town, AA/J A Tims; **80/1** View from Fortress of St Nicholas ruins, Mandraki Harbour, AA/J A Tims; **82/3** Old Town Moat, Rhodes Town, AA/J A Tims; **83** Theatre on Monte Smith Hill, AA/J A Tims; **84** Statue of Aphrodite bathing in the Archaeological Museum, Rhodes Town, AA/J A Tims; **84/5** Museum of Decorative Arts, AA/J A Tims; **86/7** Byzantine Museum, Rhodes Town, AA/J A Tims; **87** Cafes, patisseries in New Market, New Town, AA/J A Tims; **88/9** Medieval Town of Rhodes and the Church of Agia Triada, AA/J A Tims; **89** Pebbled road surface, Old Town of Rhodes, AA/S Day; **90** View looking over the Old Town Walls, Rhodes Town, AA/J A Tims; **91** Grave stone at Tzami tou Mourad Reis cemetery, Rhodes Town, AA/J A Tims; **92** View of Tzami tou Mourad Reis cemetery, Rhodes Town, AA/J A Tims; **103** Ixia, AA/S Day; **104t** Traganou beach along Afantou Bay, AA/J A Tims; **104b** Locals playing Backgammon in village of Afantou Bay, AA/J A Tims; **104/5** View looking over Castle ruins in Archangelos, AA/J A Tims; **106** Narrow street, Emponas, AA/J A Tims; **106/7** The Seven Springs at Epta Piges, AA/D Hannigan; **108** Faliraki nightlife, AA/J A Tims; **108/9t** Faliraki beach, AA/J A Tims; **108/9b** Looking over the Bay of Charaki, AA/J A Tims; **110/1** Ixia, AA/T L Carlsen; **112** The church at Kremasti, AA/D Hannigan; **112/3** Pebble floor, Church of the Panagia, Kremasti, AA/J A Tims; **113t** Fortified Kastro, village of Kritinia, AA/S Day; **113b** View over countryside from Kritinia Castle, AA/J A Tims; **114** Ladiko, AA/J A Tims; **115** Beach, Stegna, AA/J A Tims; **117** View from summit of Profitis Ilias mountain, AA/J A Tims; **118/9t** Boat under construction in Charani Bay on the island of Symi, AA/S Day; **118/9b** Harbour at Symi, AA/D Hannigan; **120** Bell tower of the Taxiarchas Michael Panormitis Monastery, AA/D Hannigan; **122/3** The church of Megali Panagia, Symi Town, AA/D Hannigan; **124/5** Thermes Kalithea, AA/D Hannigan; **125** Trianta, AA/J A Tims; **131** Castle of the Knights of St John, Lindos, AA/S Day; **132/3** Sunset over Chalki and other islands from just above Lakki, AA/J A Tims; **133t** Gennadi, AA/J A Tims; **133b** View over sea to Glystra beach, AA/J A Tims; **134** Fresco in a church in the village of Katavia, AA/T L Carlsen; **134/5t** Harbour at Kiotari, AA/D Hannigan; **134/5b** Restaurant, Lachania, AA/J A Tims; **136t** Lardos, AA/J A Tims; **136b** View of town, bay and Acropolis in Lindos, AA/J A Tims; **136/7** Souvenirs for sale, AA/J A Tims; **137** Entrance to the Knights Castle, Lindos AA/J A Tims; **138/9** View over the ruins of the Necropolis, Lindos AA/J A Tims; **139** St Paul's Bay beach, Lindos, AA/J A Tims; **140** Church of the Assumption of our Lady, Lindos, AA/J A Tims; **140/1** Fresco in the Church of the Assumption of our Lady in Lindos, AA/J A Tims; **141** Captain's House, Lindos, AA/J A Tims; **142** Detail of religious fresco at the Moni Thari Monastery, AA/J A Tims; **142/3t** Grape vine in the grounds of Moni Thari Monastery, AA/J A Tims; **142/3b** Monastery of the Archangel Michael at Thari, AA/D Hannigan; **143** Beach at Pefkoi, AA/J A Tims; **144** Beach, Plimiri, AA/J A Tims; **144/5** Harbour, Plimiri, AA/J A Tims; **145** Cape Akra Praso in Prasonisi, AA/J A Tims; **146/7** View over sea to Glystra beach, AA/J A Tims; **148t** Agios Pandeliemon Church, Siana, AA/J A Tims; **148b** Church of Ag Panteleimon, Siana, AA/S Day; **148/9** View above Vlika beach, AA/J A Tims.

Every effort has been made to trace the copyright holders, and we apologize in advance for any accidental errors. We would be happy to apply the corrections in the following edition of this publication.

Sight Locator Index

This index relates to the maps on the covers. We have given map references to the main sights in the book. Grid references in italics indicate sights featured on the town plan. Some sights within towns may not be plotted on the maps.

Rhodes Town M24

Anaktoro ton Arkhonton (Palace of the Grand Masters) *Rhodes Town d5*

Astiki Pinakothiki (Municipal Art Gallery) *Rhodes Town e5*

Dhimotika Loutra (Municipal Baths) *Rhodes Town d7*

Enydreio (Aquarium) *Rhodes Town c1*

Evraikis Sinikias (Old Jewish Quarter) *Rhodes Town f7*

Ippoton (Street of the Knights) *Rhodes Town d6*

Limani Mandrakiou (Mandraki Harbour) *Rhodes Town d4*

Meseoniki Tafros Rodou (Old Town Moat) *Rhodes Town c6*

Monte Smith *Rhodes Town a8*

Mouseio Archaiologiko (Archaeological Museum) *Rhodes Town d6*

Mouseio tis Kosmikis Technis (Museum of Decorative Arts) *Rhodes Town d6*

Mouseio Vizantino (Byzantine Museum) *Rhodes Town e6*

Nea Poli (New Town) *Rhodes Town d5*

Palia Poli (Old Town) *Rhodes Town e6*

Paralia tis 'Ellis (Elli Beach) *Rhodes Town c2*

Tihi tis Polis (Old Town Walls) *Rhodes Town d8*

Tzami Rejep Pascha *Rhodes Town d7*

Tzami Souleiman *Rhodes Town d6*

Tzami Sultan Mustafa *Rhodes Town d7*

Tzami Tou Mourad Reis *Rhodes Town d3*

Rhodes Island

Afandou **K20**

Akropoli, Lindos **J15**

Archangelos **K18**

Asklipio **F5**

Chalki **B12 (inset)**

Embonas **D9**

Epta Piges **K19**

Faliraki **L21**

Gennadi **E4**

Glystra **G15**

Haraki **J17**

Ialyssos **K23**

Ixia **L23**

Kamiros **E12**

Kastrou Monolithos **B7**

Kattavia **C3**

Kiotari **F5**

Kolimbia **K19**

Kremasti **K23**

Kritinia Kastellos **C10**

Ladiko **L21**

Lahania **D3**

Lardos **H15**

Lindos **J15**

Moni Thari **E7**

Pefkos **J15**

Petaloudes **J21**

Plimiri **D2**

Prasonisi **B1**

Profitis Ilias **F10**

Siana **C7**

Stegna **K18**

Symi **M24 (off map)**

Thermes Kalitheas **M22**

Trianda **K23**

Tsambika **K19**

Vlicha **J16**